And So I Kept Living

Jane + Jerry –
So grateful for
both of you!
Grace and
peace,
Ellen

Ellen Crawford True

Parson's Porch Books

www.parsonsporchbooks.com

And So I Kept Living

ISBN: Softcover 978-1-951472-21-4

Copyright © 2019 by Ellen Crawford True

And So I Kept Living

For Dave and Abby

Acknowledgements

I want to express my gratitude for everyone who is a part of this incredible adventure of life and ministry.

Thank you to the saints in the congregations where I have served, including Christ Presbyterian Church in Camp Hill, PA where these sermons were preached.

I am grateful for my mom, "The Jude" who always wondered what I would do with my "outside voice." Both she and my father as well as and my brother, George have consistently encouraged and supported this calling that none of us saw coming.

I give thanks for my lifelong friends who cheer me on, cheer me up, and keep me from taking myself too seriously. Especially, I want to thank my brilliant friend, Helen, who found time to proof and read every word.

I cannot imagine doing ministry without my phenomenal colleagues in the Well, a preaching group that is so much more. Many of their thoughts and words are scattered through these sermons.

And I want to thank my husband Dave and my daughter Abby who patiently put up with countless long Saturdays while sermons are finished and worried over.

God has given me a tremendous gift in calling me to do what I love day in and day out. I am eternally grateful.

Contents

Sermons Matter

Parson's Porch Books is delighted to present to you this series called Sermons Matter.

We believe that many of the best writers are pastors who take the role of preacher seriously. Week in, and week out, they exegete scripture, research material, write and deliver sermons in the context of the life of their particular congregation in their given community.

We further believe that sermons are extensions of Holy Scripture which need to be published beyond the manuscripts which are written for delivery each Sunday. Books serve as a vehicle for the sermon to continue to proclaim the Good News of the Morning to a broader audience.

We celebrate the wonderful occasion of the preaching event in Christian worship when the Pastor speaks, the People listen and the Work of the Church proceeds.

Take, Read, and Heed.

David Russell Tullock, M.Div., D.Min.
Publisher
Parson's Porch Books

Holy Pushback
Genesis 1:1-2:3

September 10, 2017

I think I have mentioned to some of you that my flag football team in seminary found its name in this text. We were in our first year of seminary, completely geeked out and stressed out trying to figure out how to make sense of these ancient words in unfamiliar tongue. While the traditional path is for first year students to take Greek and then New Testament, my full-of-myself self-insisted on doing things in order, first things first, so I found myself sitting among mostly second year students that blazing hot summer in Richmond, Virginia learning the basics of Hebrew. At some point we opened up the text to the beginning, just as you're supposed to, and started working our way through Genesis. It was then that we came upon a favorite vocabulary word—*tohu-wa-bohu*. This term is the one translated here as "without shape or form" and in other places as "formless and void." It is also understood to mean chaos, and as you may have guessed, it became our team name. And as time would tell, sadly we very much lived up to our name.

Chaos feels very real right about now. One part of the country is battling blazing fires, others are still waiting for the water to recede, while others are bracing for the wind and the water still to come. The chaos doesn't end at our borders, of course. A devastating earthquake struck Mexico, famine rages in Yemen, and an estimated 80 million people have been impacted by flooding in South Asia. Chaos hits closer to home, too. All chaos breaks loose with the late-night phone call, the diagnosis, the pink slip. And we begin to wonder where exactly God might be in the midst of it all.

A friend commented in the past few days that the hurricanes and fires and earthquakes are God's way of getting our attention, a divine—if horribly spiteful—wake up call. But I don't understand God that way. This text is our first introduction to the God of Israel, the Lord of the Universe, and the God we meet in this text is not the cause of the chaos but the one creating life in the midst of the chaos. This text is not a play-by-play of what happened when the world began. This is not a firsthand or eyewitness account jotted down by a court reporter. This is a story generations in the making. This is a narrative shared around campfires and family dinner tables as the people of Israel came to understand the truth of who they are and whose they are. This is a faith statement, written down by people of faith in the midst of one of Israel's most difficult and chaotic moments, moments when faith is hard to come by, moments when faith may be all there is left.

Following the destruction of the Temple and the collapse of the monarchy, the remaining Israelites are sent into exile. No familiar landmarks remain. No power to change their own fate lies within their grasp. And yet, the Spirit leads them to push back against the chaos with poetry. These sacred words point not to the chaos but to the God who insists on making a way in the midst of that chaos. This God insists that creation was—and still is—good, because God has made a way for creation, for life by pushing back against the chaos and the darkness. In the words of my friend and colleague Meg Peery McLaughlin:

> As it was then, and as it is now, when God creates,
> there is so much chaos, and darkness mounts around monsters
> and yet God's spirit hovers and stirs,
> And God speaks—and there is light. The darkness is no longer so dark.
> And God speaks—and there is sky. The *tohu-wa-bohu* is pushed up.
> And God speaks—and there is land. The *tohu-wa-bohu* is pushed down.

And God speaks—and there are creatures that crawl, and fruit that grows, and stars that shine, life that erupts in the middle of the *tohu-wa-bohu*.

God speaks—and you and I take our breath. [1]

She continues:

> Friends, we live and move and have our being in this tension between God's swirling spirit and constant chaos…I am still struck by the image in the *Washington Post* of two black men: the Rev. Willis Johnson and a teenager named Joshua Wilson. It was in the midst of Ferguson chaos…Joshua, holy fury set in his jaw, was standing his ground as police pushed down. Rev. Johnson stepped into the breach. He wrapped his arms around Joshua's body. Rev. Johnson said: 'I just embraced him because he was so angry, and you could feel it in his body. You could feel it in his speech. And I have a newly turned teenager and I've been Joshua before *and something just said, grab him, hold him.*' It seems to me that Rev. Johnson's arms were like God's, pushing back the *tohu wa bohu* for a moment, making a path for order amidst the chaos. Rev. Johnson said: 'People who are hurting need to be affirmed in their hurt. People who are angry need to be affirmed in their anger. I needed that as much as he needed that. We kept each other from harm's way. We held space for life.'[2]

We held space for life. I've been Joshua in my own way. I'm guessing you have, too. While I have not suffered the stings of poverty or racism, I have known what it is to stare my own brand of chaos in the face, and I happen to know that many of you have, too. I have told you that my

---

[1] From her paper for The Well, 2017. Meg points out that the same Hebrew word means spirit and wind.

[2] http://www.npr.org/2014/08/14/340422502/ferguson-pastor-this-is-not-a-race-issue-this-is-a-human-issue, as cited by Meg Peery McLaughlin in her paper.

mother's cancer came back right after I graduated Davidson. With my little life in a tailspin, I found myself visiting churches as I traveled with a friend in Europe. Somehow in the midst of that trip, something—or more accurately—*someone* grabbed me and held me. I was embraced by the God who knew my pain, my anger, and my confusion. This God gave me room to cry and thrash and rage against the chaos even while the God of life held space for me, calling forth life for me, eventually allowing me to see a way forward, a way that led me to ministry.

We often feel helpless when the world is turned upside down. We are overwhelmed by images of lives in turmoil and homes washed away, of cities and forests burning, of communities divided and in turmoil. We worry and we pray, and we wonder what we can do. The chaos looms so large. The chaos seems certain to win. But *tohu-wa-bohu* does not win. Not on the football field. Not in creation. We worship a God who is not daunted by the chaos, who is not stopped by the *tohu-wa-bohu*. Now and in the coming days, weeks, and months, we who have been created in the image of this God are being called to be God-like for and with other image-bearers from around the corner, across the river, down the road, and a world away. We who have been created in God's image are being called upon to hold space for life in the face of fires, floods, storms, natural disasters and disasters of humanity's own making. There are some who are tempted to see God as the author of the chaos; I do not. There are some who are tempted to claim to know the mind of God, to know why Harvey struck when he did, to know why Irma is bearing down where she is; I do not. There are some who will fixate on the chaos itself, placing it on some unholy pedestal; by the grace of God, I will not. The chaos is relentless, and yet we worship a God who is relentless, too. More relentless, in fact. This God steps into the chaos time and time again to hold space for life and declares it to be good. This is the God we worship, and this is the God whose image we bear.

I see this holy push-back, this life-building, space-saving work in our own Presbyterian Disaster Assistance. The second the rumblings of a disaster churn up PDA is on the ground working with local agencies to plan for recovery before the storms begin. They were on the ground before Harvey hit. They are standing at the ready in the wake of Irma and Jose even now. These image-bearers, these beloved children of God, these volunteers do their part to rebuild homes and lives around the corner and around the world. Their tagline reads: "Out of chaos. Hope." You can only begin to usher in hope when you can stare down the chaos first. Their work and witness in the midst of devastation point to this God who makes and holds a space for life even in the bleakest of places and in the most difficult of times. They push back with sweat and shovels. They push back with prayers and their very presence.

We are part of God's good creation, but unlike the crawling and clip-clopping creatures, we and all of our fellow human beings are made in God's image. We alone have the ability and the responsibility to push back against chaos and destruction when we can and where we can, against everything that would harm creation and our fellow creatures. And so we push back, too. We push back with buckets and bugspray. We push back with listening to those who are different from us and learning from those who have a different viewpoint or experience from ours. We push back when we seek to make peace and find a new way forward through the chaos of racism and injustice. We push back by refusing to worship and fixate on the chaos. We push back when we refuse to believe that the chaos will win. We push back when we worship the God of life, the One who pushes back for us, the One who holds space for us, the One who stands in the breech even now, the One who looks on creation and still insists that it is good.

Amen.

This Side of Eden
Genesis 2 and 3, selected verses

September 11, 2016

We begin our new year with an old story, one we could probably tell without reading it. We know the characters: God, Adam, Eve, the snake, the tree, and of course that forbidden fruit. It's a familiar story, too familiar perhaps, one that has been imagined and re-imagined throughout the centuries by great authors like John Milton and great theologians like Augustine and the even the writers of *Desperate Housewives.* So as we begin our walk through the Old Testament this fall, I invite you to listen as I read from Genesis 2 and 3 and maybe, just maybe, together we'll hear a fresh word from this ancient text. [Read Genesis 2:4b-9, 15-17; 3:1-13, 20-23]

This second creation account is different from the first one, the "In the beginning" one. Here we find no grand cosmic vision, no orderly day-by-day account of God's creating ways. Instead our vision is dialed down to the creative act as a messy one, a dirty one. God gathers up dirt—*adamah* in Hebrew, and forms Adam (*adam* in Hebrew). God will go on to do the same thing with the other creatures, shaping them from the dirt at his feet and parading them past the man to see what kind of partner might be a true helper in the dirty work of living in this new creation, the dirty work of tending the new earth. The one difference between the human and the other creatures is that God's breath pours into the man's lungs. The human carries God's breath, God's spirit inside him. God takes special care to create a partner with whom God can work, a partner who can be entrusted with tending God's beloved soil and cultivating God's treasured garden. God wants the partner to have a partner of his own, too, one who is suitable to share the work and the joy of being God's breath-bearing creatures in

God's new world. And so God creates Eve out of his most treasured creation, Adam.

Over the centuries, Eve has captured the imagination more than some other biblical figures. It's understandable. She is the focus of the action in the story after all, the one who chats with the snake, the one whose thoughts we overhear, the one who dares to reach for that wisdom-bearing fruit first. Eve is certainly more interesting than Adam. We don't hear much from him, after all, but we get to hear *her* thoughts. The text tells us that Eve's interest in eating the fruit arises from the promise of wisdom. We think of wisdom as a trait developed over years of living and learning. We might blame Eve for looking for a shortcut, but can we really blame her? Adam will, of course, but if the opportunity to know more, even *all*, presented itself, can we honestly say that we would have left that apple (or pear or pomegranate or peach) just hanging there? The text does not portray her as a seductress or reduce her to a manipulating caricature. The text tells us: "She also gave some to her husband, who was with her, and he ate."[3] So I'm not sure I really blame Eve for taking that bite, and for all of the heat she's received over the centuries, I'm not sure the original writers of Genesis blame her either.

We want someone to blame though. We always do. We always have. It's a tale as old as time, as is our universal longing for a time or a place untouched by disappointment, anger, frailty, strife, or danger. Even though we know that Genesis is not a play-by-play of humanity's first days, we are still tempted to wonder what it would be like if we could turn back time, to imagine what life would be like if Eve had a do-over and chose to ignore the snake and go on about her day. What would life be like if we were still in that garden? We'll never know. The writers of Genesis never knew either, of course. We've never set foot in that garden; nor did they. I've heard it said that we cannot miss what we

---

[3] Genesis 3: 6, NRSV

never knew. And yet we do, at least in this case. We always have, it seems. Apparently, we have been grieving this lost paradise for as long as humans have been able to look around and see that things are not as they could be or should be. So this grief is nothing new, but in a post-Hiroshima world, a post-Holocaust world, a post-9/11 world, our grieving for paradise lost, for a perfect world grows deeper, more vivid, as does the temptation to find someone to blame.

And we have always looked for someone to blame for our being kicked out of paradise, for someone to blame for our not being able to get back there. In fact this old, old story could just be written off as an origin story for why human beings started pointing fingers and looking for a scapegoat, or scape-snake to take the fall for our mistakes, but my hunch is that there is more to it than that. While the creation story gets very little attention in the rest of the Old Testament, it is still central to how we and our ancient Hebrew ancestors understand ourselves, and it is crucial to how we and our ancient Hebrew ancestors understand our relationship with our Creator.

From the beginning, God wants what is best for humanity. The humans are created for relationship with each other, with the creation, and with God, the generous and gracious Creator. The writer points out that every tree is theirs for the taking, every tree except one. The only restraint God places on the humans is that they do not eat from the tree of the knowledge of good and evil. There are all sorts of arguments about what the tree represents and why there are two named trees at one point and only one at another. But in the end, God draws a line, God shows the humans that line, and they choose to cross it; we choose to cross it. We may resist hearing that lines or boundaries are there for our own good. We do not like to hear that there are limits to what we can know, limits to what we are able to handle, limits built into our very being. We carry God's breath, but we are not God. We cannot handle the truth that comes with even a taste of divine wisdom. When our eyes fly open, we are shocked to discover just how not like

God we are. We are overwhelmed by our vulnerability, by how exposed we are. This is not a story about sexuality gone awry or about some Victorian notion of bodies being bad, dirty, or sinful. *God does not tell them to cover up, after all.* When Eve and Adam's eyes are opened, they do not die immediately, but their innocence does. Their grabbing for the closest fig leaf is less about their bodies and more about fear of vulnerability, the terror of standing exposed before their Creator and the entire creation. Before they crossed the line and took that bite, they had nothing to hide. Now they do. We do. And yet they cannot hide from God. Nor can we.

Perhaps my favorite moment in the text comes when God walks in the garden. I love the idea of the Creator of the Universe taking an evening stroll, enjoying the wonders of date trees and rabbits. God's footsteps are a familiar sound it seems. Maybe on other evenings Adam and Eve have run toward the Lord God and shared the events of the day. This time is different, though. At the familiar sound of those footsteps, Eve and Adam's ears perk up, and like children who spilled a can of purple paint on the white living room rug, their first instinct is to hide in fear. First, they hide, and then they blame. And blame some more. Using the divine breath which fills their lungs, the humans give no direct answers, only dodges and finger pointing. "She made me do it," he says. "It made me do it," she says. And in the same breath, God wonders aloud, "What have the two of you done?" Not "gotcha!" Not "busted!" Not "go to your room!" or "you're grounded!" or "just wait till your mother gets home!" Instead, the Creator, with sighs too deep for words, asks, "What have you done?" We are not the only ones who grieve what has been lost. Now it seems that the Creator grieves, too.

While Eve may capture our imagination, it is God who captures the story, because it is God who moves the humans off the hamster-wheel blame game and into life beyond paradise. It is God after all, who turns dressmaker and gives the pair something sturdier than fig leaves to wear out in the world, outfitting them for post-Eden world where there is still earth to be cultivated and work to be done. The Creator takes care to dress them to live in that world. Even as God ushers these two out of paradise, God is faithful still.

Walker Marsh has never lived in paradise. In fact he spends much of his time in a place many would say is the opposite of Eden, a blighted section of Baltimore where "boarded-up rowhouses line the streets and weeds flourish in sidewalk cracks."[4] With a grant and a vision, Marsh started Tha Flower Factory, an urban flower garden that raises flowers for florists, a café, and area neighbors. Among the "bright yellow sunflowers, purple salvia, pink phlox and red day lilies [Marsh also grows] cabbage, peppers and tomatoes" and gives them away to neighbors for free.[5] One neighbor, Andre Matthews can't say enough about the ways Marsh's flowers have helped transform the neighborhood. He calls Marsh's creation:

> 'a paradise in the jungle.' [Matthews remembers] when [the] neighborhood [was] nothing — just abandoned buildings, then after those were torn down, nothing but weeds and bricks and rocks…Marsh brought it back to life.[6]

Marsh is humble about his impact, but he does recognize that the project offers a sign of hope. He found freedom in getting his hands dirty, in working to bring beauty from the dust, new life in a written-off place, far from any dreams of a perfect paradise. In hiring 20 growers to work alongside him, he hopes that others might find the same joy he has. Marsh is not pining away for paradise lost; he's working to bring hope and beauty where he is now, in the midst of the weeds and the rocks.

---

[4] Jonathan Pitts, "A Paradise amid the Rocks and Weeds," http://www.baltimoresun.com/news/maryland/baltimore-city/bs-md-tha-flower-factory-20160824-story.html
[5] Pitts
[6] Pitts

It is easy—seductive even—to dream about living in Eden, but there is more life to be lived in the outside-of-Eden world, even if it means leaving Eden—and dreams of Eden—behind. And since we have all left Eden behind, maybe it is time to build what we can, rather than grieving what we cannot. Wistful what-ifs, fixation on playing the blame game, and an insistence on pointing fingers do very little to nurture creation or honor the creator. As tempting as it is, nostalgia for a golden age does little to redeem today. Lest we forget, as God's own, we are in the creation and redemption game. We are created to partner with God in tending creation; that has not changed. Maybe it's time to stop fixating on who is to blame. Maybe it's time to stop hiding in fear. Maybe it is our turn to roll up our divinely sewn sleeves and get a little dirty. Maybe it's time for us to get back to the holy work of cultivating hope in the midst of rocks and weeds in name of the Creator who walks among us, the One who delights in us still, the One who remains faithful always.

In the name of the Father and of the Son and of the Holy Spirit. Amen.

The Blessing Business
Genesis 28: 10-22

September 24, 2017

After last week's text, we hear only a little more about Abraham. The focus shifts to Isaac and to Abraham's other descendants. Isaac grows up and marries Rebekah. After struggling with infertility, Isaac and Rebekah discover they are expecting twins, but the pregnancy is not an easy one. Scripture tells us that "The children struggled together within her" and that the struggle was painful enough to make her wonder why she survived. She asked God what to make of this battle within her, and God's response was a difficult one:

> 'Two nations are in your womb, and two peoples born of you shall be divided; the one shall be stronger than the other, the elder shall serve the younger.'[7]

Rebekah goes on to deliver the twins, first Esau and then Jacob grabbing Esau's heel. Even from the beginning, Jacob is grasping, grabbing. And the text tells us that each parent has a favorite. Isaac's favorite is Esau; Rebekah's favorite is Jacob. He tricks Esau into giving away his birthright—the rights of the elder son—for a bowl of stew. And then Rebekah guides Jacob in stealing Esau's blessing from Isaac as well, essentially making him the firstborn son, the one who will inherit all that had been planned for Esau. As you may recall, Isaac sends Esau to hunt for supper promising to bless his elder son before Isaac dies. Rebekah devises a plan where she cooks a meal for Isaac and encourages Jacob to feed it to his father, wearing goat skins on his arms and neck so that his skin will appear to be as hairy as Esau's. Isaac questions if the son in front of him is truly Esau but goes ahead and blesses Jacob anyway. Moments later, Esau returns to discover that his

---

[7] Genesis 25:23, NRSV

father's blessing cannot be undone, nor can it be duplicated. There is one blessing, and Jacob the grasping one has grabbed it for himself. Esau plans to kill Jacob. Rebekah sends Jacob away to find a wife and to save his life. Now on the run and far from all he knows, Jacob stops to rest for the evening. [Read Genesis 28:10-22]

Ancestry and genealogy are quite the rage these days. Send in a small sample and a lab can tell you where you come from. The ads on television make the whole process sound so exciting, so exotic. I'm fairly certain that there are not a lot of surprises in my DNA. Mine is a fairly generic combo of English, Irish, and German with maybe a little French thrown in. But as I visited with relatives on my dad's side recently, I was still struck by seeing that shared DNA at work. I saw family traits writ large in front of me. My cousin and I inherited our great grandmother's hazel eyes. It looks like we may both have gotten our grandmother's cheeks, too. When I'm sore or sleepy, I start to shuffle like my dad and his dad. I've been told I have my mother's hands. The family traits are being passed down as well. One of my cousin's daughters is her mother's spitting image. Abby's geometry teacher took one look at me on Back-to-School Night and knew exactly whose mother I was. We come by these things honestly, don't we? These traits and mannerisms are in our genes, our DNA. They are a big part of how we're made.

Jacob takes after his family, too. While he may have his mother's eyes or his father's smile, that blessing is the most noticeable thing handed down to him. Except he does not come by that honestly, does he? He tricks and connives and steals the blessing right out from under Esau and Isaac. Really?! THIS guy is the bearer of the grand promise? THIS guy is the one whose name will later be changed to Israel? THIS guy is the one whose name will be synonymous with the people of God, God's chosen ones? Really?!

We shake our heads and tsk tsk, but we have a soft spot for little guys, don't we? The crafty ones? The "young, scrappy, and hungry" ones? We root for Jack Sparrow and the Bad News Bears and Danny Ocean and Robin Hood. So why not Jacob? My hunch is that whole blessing mess. The thought of God's blessing's being bestowed on one so dramatically undeserving makes us squirm a bit. Or maybe more than just a bit. Blessings come through playing by the rules and doing what we're told. Not by grasping and taking what rightfully belongs to someone else, especially when God's involved.

But what exactly does it mean to be blessed? A quick search on Twitter for that ever-present hashtag, #blessed reveals people celebrating birthdays and business successes and football victories and great seats at a Reba McEntire concert. Gifts? Yes. Reasons to be grateful? Definitely. Examples of divine blessing? I'm not so sure.

Before the divine blessing, Jacob manages to grab a blessing from his father, but that blessing means very little in the middle of nowhere. Alone in the desert, on the outs with his dysfunctional family, and running for his life, Jacob stops for the night with nothing but a rock to tuck under his head. One would think that this would lead to a fretful night's sleep, if sleep comes at all, but Jacob not only sleeps, he dreams. And in that dream, this on-the-lam scoundrel encounters the living God and a ladder stretched to heaven on which the angels climb and descend. It's not Jacob's ladder, but a holy ladder bridging heaven and earth. And then God stands beside him and declares him blessed. God meets Jacob at his most vulnerable and blesses him. But this is not like Isaac's blessing. Nor is it anything like the ones claimed on Twitter. Inherent in God's blessing is a crucial piece that the hashtag seems to miss. God blesses Abraham and Jacob in order to bless others, in order to bring blessings to the world through them. To be blessed is to be in the business of blessing. You can't have one without the other.

And whether he realizes it or not, blessing is who Jacob is. It's how he's made. It's deeper than his DNA. It has been since God called his granddaddy to leave everything and everyone he knew to start anew. This blessing business does not mean he's arrived. This blessing business means he's only getting started. Jacob doesn't earn God's blessing, and by our standards he certainly does not deserve it. But the blessing is his, and so this trickster is suddenly in the family business, the blessing business himself. And he has a lot to learn about what that means.

In the next few verses, Jacob tries to set the terms of the covenant, the terms of the blessing. But his terms are too narrow; his notion of blessing too small. He drills down on a full belly and a shirt on his back so that he can return to his own father's house. God has something much bigger in mind. God's concern transcends any one family, any one tribe, or any one nation. This family business is not contained to one family. To be blessed is to be in the blessing business, and to be in the blessing business is to follow God beyond his own backyard, beyond his own zip code, beyond his own borders. To be in the blessing business is to have his eyes and his world blown wide open.

In the wake of Harvey a reporter wandered through some Houston neighborhoods talking to residents about what they had managed to save. That's when he met Shirley Hines. Ms. Hines was grateful to have found a broken Fitz and Floyd coffee cup. Ms. Hines said:

> These cups belong to my mother [who died in 2000] …She just had them sitting on the cabinet in the kitchen, because she would drink coffee out of them occasionally. When I was really down, I'd get one and drink me some coffee.[8]

---

[8] https://www.nytimes.com/2017/09/05/us/treasures-saved-harvey.html?_r=0

All of the white china cups with red bands were broken. Not one could hold a cup of coffee now. Hundreds of miles away, Ann Dahm read Ms. Hines's story and felt compelled to act. She called the Fitz and Floyd headquarters to see if they had any cups in that pattern in their inventory. They said that pattern hadn't been in use since 1979, but they tracked down three for purchase elsewhere. Ms. Dahm purchased the cups and had them shipped to Texas. She told the reporter:

> I desperately wanted to replace that broken cup. The world is a broken place, but also a place of great strength, dignity, and personal courage. That's what I wanted to honor.[9]

Ms. Hines was deeply touched by the gift. One cup—or even three—won't rebuild Ms. Hines's world, but that one small act does remind her that she is beloved—blessed even—in the midst of all that has been lost. All because a sibling she never knew saw her in her pain and found a way to bring bit of healing, a bit of blessing in the midst of a broken world.

I do not know why some lose their homes to hurricanes while others do not. I do not know why some children are born into happy homes while others are not. I do not know why some struggle in an endless cycle of poverty or violence while others do not. In the end I don't really think it's a case being deserving or not, nor do I think it has much if anything to do with being blessed or not. I do not know why good people struggle and thieves like Jacob wind up the father of nations. But I do know this. We who know the love of this fiercely faithful God are blessed beyond measure. And we who are blessed are called to join the family business, the blessing business, to open our eyes and our hearts to be a blessing to others. That's what this blessing business is all about after all: participating in God's larger hopes and dreams and

---

[9] https://www.nytimes.com/2017/09/11/reader-center/hurricane-harvey-teacups.html?smprod=nytcore-ipad&smid=nytcore-ipad-share

schemes for God's beloved and broken world. God creates the world good and calls humanity—God's own beloved and broken children—to join the family business, and God claims us and calls us blessed, not so that we can have something to tweet with a hashtag, but so that we can be a blessing to others. And so we who are blessed look for ways to bless our siblings in Mexico as they dig out from earthquakes and our siblings in Puerto Rico as they recover from the storm of the century. We who are blessed fill buckets for our siblings in Florida and Houston. We who are blessed welcome strangers and fight for children who are not our own. And we who are blessed find coffee cups for a grieving sister we've never met. It's deeper than our DNA. It's who we are because of whose we are. Friends, we are God's broken, beloved and blessed children, and so we are already in the blessing business.

In the name of the Father and of the Son and of the Holy Spirit. Amen.

Dream World
Genesis 37 and 50

September 25, 2016

We've covered—or flown over—a substantial amount of history between last week's text and this morning's. As you may know, Abraham and Sarah do become parents with the birth of Isaac. Isaac marries Rebekah who gives birth to twins—Esau and Jacob. Jacob comes out grasping his brother's heel and is his mother's favorite. With Rebekah's help, Jacob tricks his brother out of his birthright and fools his father into blessing him in place of Esau. Jacob wrestles with God who changes his name to Israel. This trickster Jacob goes on to be the father of twelve sons, including Joseph. [Read Genesis 37, selected verses.]

In case you didn't know, I'm an older sibling, a big sister to one younger brother. For a very long while I kept a list of the ways my brother had it better or easier than I. It's funny, as I've gotten older, the list has grown fuzzier. All I can remember now is that he got to see a PG movie at a younger age than I did, and that he got to spend the night at a friend's house earlier, too. There were many times when I insisted that my parents loved him more than me, including the time I packed a suitcase at the age of 7 and made it as far as the big boxwoods in front of the house, before deciding that it might be better to tough it out and sleep in my own bed.

So when imagining myself in this story, I am much more likely to side with the older brothers. Let's face it. Joseph is not a sympathetic character. He's a spoiled and mouthy seventeen-year-old. He is his father's favorite, not simply in his own eyes but in everyone else's, too. He sports a fancy coat that shouts his special status to the world. And then he has the nerve to talk about those dreams. It's hard to know whether he is especially cocky in that moment, or just dense.

Disney has tried to convince us that "a dream is a wish your heart makes, when you're fast asleep," but dreams in scripture are far more than a wish. This isn't about a dream vacation or Barbie's dream house, but this dream is different. Dreams like Joseph's do not come with pink puffy clouds or calming music. This dream is a window into what could be. This dream is disruptive and threatening. It turns things on their heads.

It probably doesn't help that Joseph has been such a pest. It probably doesn't help that he is so obviously his father's favorite. It doesn't help that he has spied on them for their father and tattled on them. Now he's spouting off about dreams of wheat stalks bowing to another. Maybe those wheat stalks are the last straw. But that doesn't justify the brothers' plotting to kill Joseph, does it? Isn't that a bit extreme?

Reuben thinks so, or so it seems. This older brother steps in and tries to hold off the killing part. He tries to strike a compromise, to buy time. He seems to want to save his brother, to protect him even. His plan might have worked, perhaps, if it wasn't for those angry brothers. When he returns to the cistern, the pit as it's called in other translations, he finds it empty. If his primary concern is Joseph, his response seems a bit off: "'The boy's gone! And I—where can I go now?'"[10] Somehow it suddenly becomes all about Reuben. So maybe Reuben wasn't purely concerned with Joseph's well-being after all. Perhaps he had hopes of winning Jacob's admiration if he was the one to bring Joseph home. It all gets tangled up in Reuben's mind. It becomes about him, not about the boy tossed into the cistern and sold into slavery. Rather than protect his younger brother from the hatred of the others, Reuben winds up going along, playing along. Getting rid of the dreamer and his dreams becomes the primary task, no matter what. Jacob the trickster now gets tricked himself. Reuben hands him

---

[10] Genesis 37: 30, Common English Bible

a bloody coat and inherits the family business of deception without a word.

Now I have never tossed my brother into a pit or sold him for twenty pieces of silver, but as much as I hate to admit it, I'm afraid I may have played the Reuben role, if not in my immediate family, perhaps in the larger human family. I was born in 1968, months after the death of another dreamer who died for speaking his dreams out loud. Last spring, on my last day visiting Birmingham, I touched the bars of Martin Luther King, Jr.'s jail cell, the one where he wrote his famous letter. I read that letter in high school and college. I've read it since. Each time I have bristled at King's frustration with the white moderate preachers, the ones who told King that he was moving too far, too fast in his leading the push for voting rights and civil rights. I have smugly insisted to myself that I would never have been one of those preachers. I have romanticized the Civil Rights movement and imagined myself linking arms with other clergy as they walked across that bridge in Selma or marched in the streets of Birmingham to be met by firehoses and snarling dogs. I even began to think everything had been solved, that the dream had been achieved. I confess I was living in a dream world. The events of the past few years have started to wake me up.

Numerous friends have quoted King's words back to me this past week, words about love driving out hate, words about his dream. But those words tempt me to forget that dreams are disruptive, as are the dreamers. King was not so beloved fifty-three years ago, nor was his dream. According to polls conducted in 1964:

63% of Americans said those pushing for civil rights were pushing too fast.

58% said most were violent.

58% of Americans said those pushing for civil rights were hurting their own cause.[11]

I like to think I would have been better, known better, that I would not have been among the white moderate clergy, that I would not have been Reuben, that I would not have been the one standing between the dream and its future, that I would not have been the one who opted to go along with the easier option, the less conflictual choice. I don't want to be Reuben. I don't want to be party to trying to squash a holy dream because it makes me uncomfortable or challenges the way I see the world. Reuben gave up, gave in so easily. I wonder if I would have done the same then. I worry that I'm doing the same now.

After Joseph finds his way to Pharaoh's court, through various twists and turns, his dreaming and his ability to speak the language of dreams lands him in Pharaoh's inner circle. Joseph understands that Pharaoh's dreams warn of a coming famine, so Egypt is able to store and prepare saving the lives of countless Egyptians, and even Joseph's family. Following their reunion and their father's death, the brothers wonder and worry about whether Joseph bears a grudge. [Read Genesis 50: 15-22]

I wonder what the brothers find so threatening in Joseph's dream, especially when we hear where it leads. Maybe the divisions were already too deep, the hatred too entrenched, but his dream was never about lording over them. The dream was about using his power to feed them and others, to bring life and save lives. Maybe their jealousy clouded their vision; maybe their hatred changed their listening; maybe their fear shouted down any chance of hearing what the dream might mean for them as a family and others.

---

[11] From the Southern Poverty Law Center, http://bit.ly/2diriOa

I have heard a whole array of opinions about the Black Lives Matter movement and opinions about the protests in Charlotte. Yes, there are troublemakers seizing the chance to stir the pot and incite violence, but from what I hear from friends and colleagues in Charlotte and Dallas and elsewhere, the majority are protesting peacefully, simply wanting their pain to be heard and their dreams to be listened to. Their fears are justified. Their pain is real. I have never worried about more than a traffic ticket when being pulled over. My black friends have. I have never worried about my spouse or my child being stopped for no reason other than the color of their skin. My black friends do. That said, these friends have big, real dreams, too, and our dreams are not all that different. They, too, dream of a world where all people are treasured and valued. They, too, long for a world where all are safe and fed, a world where there is peace and justice for all—not just black or brown lives, but all lives. I don't think I have listened to their fears and dreams closely enough before. Unfortunately, it has taken their dreams dying before my eyes for me to wake up from my own dream world.

I saw a photo yesterday of people gathered in a park in Charlotte. There were pop-up tents and stacks of water bottles, and a handwritten sign that read: "Today, I will listen." The hashtag asks: #areyoulisteningtoo. I hope so. I don't want to dodge it anymore. I don't want to shy away from the dream, no matter how much it may rattle my own dream world. With God's help, I am ready to listen, I am ready wake up.

While there's a challenging word in this text, there is a tremendous word of grace as well. Joseph's speech at the end offers hope, even to me:

Don't be afraid. Am I God? You planned something bad for me, but God produced something good from it, in order to save the lives of many people, just as he's doing today.[12]

Some hear an "everything-happens-for-a-reason" kind of grace in Joseph's words. Some hear that God wills all these things to happen, that God will clean up the mess we make, no matter how big. But God does not tear off Joseph's coat. God does not toss him into the pit. Joseph may forgive his brothers, but God's bringing life out of death does not excuse Reuben's cowardice or the brothers' death-dealing ways. That said, Joseph's words are full of hope and promise. There is hope for Reuben and for me if we are willing to wake up and listen. While God's saving ways may not let Reuben or me off the hook, those saving ways do invite Reuben and me to play our part in a larger dream, God's dream of life and peace and justice for all. The great good news is that we are included in God's dream. We are invited to take our place in God's dream world instead of hiding in our own.

Sounds like a dream come true.

In the name of the Father and of the Son and of the Holy Spirit. Amen.

---

[12] Genesis 50: 19-20, CEB

Getting Our Toes Wet
Exodus 14

September 30, 2018

The final verse of last week's text tells us: "Whatever Joseph did, the Lord made it prosper."[13] While in prison, Joseph catches the attention of pharaoh's household because of his gift for making sense of dreams, especially pharaoh's dreams. Under Joseph's guidance, Egypt sets aside grain and livestock during years of plenty and is well-prepared when famine strikes. Then, as you may recall, Joseph's family comes to Egypt looking for food. They do not recognize Joseph, but he works to give them what they need and eventually reconciles with them and is reunited with his father Jacob. So all is well...for a while. The beginning of the book of Exodus tells us that the Israelites thrived in Egypt and grew in strength and numbers. But then, things change. The people once welcomed as guests are now seen as a threat. A new king who has no memory of Joseph and his saving ways fears that the Israelites will side with Egypt's enemies in a time of war, so he plans to oppress and enslave them. One part of this plan includes having the male Hebrew children killed in childbirth. When that fails—thanks to some courageous midwives, the king orders that the baby boys be thrown into the Nile. And that's when we meet Moses. This baby boy is hidden by his mother in a reed basket that floats him into pharaoh's household as the adopted child of pharaoh's daughter. Moses grows up surrounded by wealth and privilege, but eventually something nudges him to protest the beating of a Hebrew slave and ultimately killing an Egyptian guard. Moses flees to the wilderness, lives as a shepherd, and meets God in a burning bush. He returns to Egypt to tell pharaoh to let God's people go. Pharaoh resists. God keeps pushing through a series of plagues and eventually, on the heels of the

---

[13] Genesis 39:23, NRSV

final plague, the death of every Egyptian first born child, pharaoh relents. The Egyptians hurry the Hebrews out of town and hand off their gold and silver, too. Then pharaoh changes his mind. [Exodus 14:5-14, 21-29]

A few weeks back, it was hard to turn away from the coverage of Hurricane Florence, or Flo as she's come to be known. One of the most powerful images was a graphic on the Weather Channel showing what a rising storm surge looks like.[14] The reporter stands in the middle of circle, and an image of rising water grows around her. It shows the power of the water at 3 feet, when the current is strong, and walking becomes difficult. Then at 6 feet the water rises above the reporter's head, over the car parked over the speaker's right shoulder and even begins to lift the car. As the water swells to nine feet, the reporter points out that the water will now flow over the top of any one-story building in its path. It's a powerful image, one that is intended to encourage anyone who would dare risk staying behind to leave. It also drives home for those of us on dry ground just what our brothers and sisters in the Carolinas were up against. It is stunning to see how quickly one human being is dwarfed by this wall of water, water that almost entirely surrounds her. But that water is no more than a graphic on a green screen, a make-believe threat that she can leave behind with the click of a button. It's a different story when the water is real.

That image of water towering overhead makes me even more sympathetic to the grumbling Israelites. They are newly free and newly wealthy. Life should be good, but now, at God's command Moses wants them to move into the sea, and they do not swim. Water means chaos and the unknown. They are stuck between Egypt's world-class army and the sea, and they understandably protest. They know what it is to live as slaves in Egypt. They know how to make bricks. On their good days, they know how to avoid the taskmaster's wrath. On their

---

[14] https://youtu.be/bRkXPuGAHkE

not-so-good days they know how to endure that wrath. Their vision is skewed. As another preacher says:

> Their rose-colored glasses have erased the memories of being enslaved, of being persecuted, of having their children thrown into the Nile, of being abused by their Egyptian taskmasters.[15]

The water distorts their vision yet again. They are terrified by the unknown that lies ahead, and they begin to romanticize what they have left behind. Maybe it wasn't so bad. Maybe if they wave the white flag, pharaoh will let bygones be bygones and let them get back to brick-making. But God wants more for them. God wants to lead them out of slavery and into life. It seems so straightforward to us. We know how the story goes. We know that sea will not overwhelm them, but they do not. They cannot see the new thing God is doing in front of them. All they can see is water. All. That. Water. And the angry empire breathing down their necks. And so they look back, and long for what they had—or what they now think they had. They do not even want to dip a toe in to that swirling sea. They cannot imagine how anything good could come of that. Except, perhaps, for Nachshon.

There is a story from the midrash, a story the rabbis told about this moment, recorded in the Talmud, the Jewish teachings about scripture. In this story, the Israelites hear the order from God: "Go forward." ...and they look at the roiling sea and hesitate. The pillar of fire and cloud move behind them, separating them from the Egyptians, so they can no longer look back. They can only look at the sea. Moses stretches out his hand, and the Israelites look at the sea...until a man called Nachshon, brother-in-law of Aaron, the brother of Moses and Miriam, takes the first step. He walks into the sea, up to his ankles...up to his knees...he keeps walking, and the people watch...up to his waist, up to

---

[15] The Rev. Teri Peterson in her sermon found here:
https://clevertitlehere.blogspot.com/2018/09/forward-in-faitha-sermon-on-crossing.html

his chest...still he walks forward in faith. Up to his shoulders, up to his chin... [when he is in up to his nostrils] the waters part, and he stands on dry ground, going on, just as God had called. He goes forward and the way appears, and the whole body of the Israelites walk across, with a wall of water on one side and the other.[16]

This story is not in the scripture we receive, and yet, it is true that in Red Sea moments like this one, someone has to go first. So I find myself wondering what gives someone like Nachshon the courage to step forward first into the water. I watched that virtual wall of water surround the Weather Channel reporter, and I found myself frustrated with those who still would not leave. All I could see was the water that would soon tower above stop signs and mailboxes. Because I had seen that water before. We lived in eastern North Carolina in 1999 when Floyd blew through. Before the storm hit, I was frantically—and naively—on the phone with the world's most patient state trooper while she calmly explained that it was a bad idea for me to try to take my college students to Montreat in the western part of the state for a retreat. I could not envision just how bad it would get, just how difficult it would be to get out and back in, let alone how hard it would be to get students back to their families and out of harm's way. But I did what she told me to. I stayed put and watched the waters rise.

I have never seen a sky as blue as the one overhead after the winds died down. It was sunny and beautiful, like everything had been washed clean. And then the waters came. Our house was spared, but the water filled streams and rivers and eventually streets undaunted by any barriers. It was hard to see anything other than water, and it was nearly impossible to imagine that anything good could come in its wake. But then the Nachshons arrived. They wore waders and donated

---

[16] As re-told by the Rev. Teri Peterson, https://clevertitlehere.blogspot.com/2018/09/forward-in-faitha-sermon-on-crossing.html

clothes and cooked hot meals and offered hugs and sat and wept with those who had lost everything. And not once did I hear them disparage the ones who had stayed behind. Because anyone who found their way into eastern North Carolina that fall saw what the water could do, what the water had done, especially to the lives of those who were barely able to stay afloat even before the first drop of rain fell.

It is so easy to shake my head at the Israelites when they hesitate at the sea's edge. They should know better. They should get out. And yet, they have no way to imagine life outside of slavery. Their vision is clouded by generations of oppression. They have forgotten that the empire cannot be trusted. They have forgotten that God can. They cannot see the new thing God promises to do, because all they can see is water.

I'm guessing you've had moments like this, moments when you have stood between the old life that led only to dead ends and the new life in the unknown ahead. What or who gave you the courage to walk forward? Because walk forward you did. Somehow you put one foot in front of the other. Somehow you found a way to trust—even for a moment—that the walls of water on either side could be trusted to hold, that the God who built them could build something new in you, too.

There are many who are trapped between the old life and the new even now: flood survivors who are knee deep in the business of mucking out; survivors of abuse whose pain is ridiculed or dismissed; immigrants who have left behind family, customs, language, and culture because their village is no longer home; foster children who carry all they own from one temporary home to another in garbage bags; opioid addicts whose lives—and those of their families—teeter on the brink. Who will be Nachshon for them? Who will step forward in faith and invite them to come, too? My hope is that it will be the church. My hope is that we will speak God's holy words of promise instead of the empire's language of disdain. My hope is that we will show what it means to trust not the mighty chariots of pharaoh, but the faithfulness of a God who makes a way through the sea. Because at some point along the way, we have been stuck, too, and God refused to leave us there. When we were beaten down, written off, or paralyzed by fear, God fought for us. We who have passed through the dangerous waters of baptism, who have trudged through the mud, who have been welcomed into new life, just may be the very ones called to be Nachshon here and now. Maybe it's time to get our toes wet so that others can walk forward on God's dry ground, too.

In the name of the Father and of the Son and of the Holy Spirit. Amen.

Character(s) Welcome
1 Samuel 16: 1-13

October 20, 2013

In the chapters between last week's lesson and today's, Israel pleads with God for a king, a human king like the ones their neighbors have. After warning Israel about the hazards to trading a human king for a divine one, God instructs Samuel to anoint Saul as Israel's first king. The narrator tells us, "There was not a man among the people of Israel more handsome than Saul; he stood head and shoulders above everyone else."[17] This striking young man is called and set apart to save God's people from their enemies. Not all of Israelites are convinced at first, nor is Saul who keeps Samuel's words to him a secret and tries to hide from Samuel when it is time to present him as God's chosen one. After a successful military victory, Saul is universally embraced as king, at least for a little while. In the chapter that precedes our reading for today, we are told that God regrets making Saul king.[18] As our passage begins, Saul remains king, but his days are numbered. Samuel is angry and heartbroken. [Read 1 Samuel 16: 1-13]

In recent years, the USA Network has enticed new viewers with the tag line: "Characters welcome," celebrating the uniqueness and quirkiness of the characters on their shows. One thing we have discovered and rediscovered over the course of seven weeks in the Old Testament this fall is that scripture, the sacred text in which the word of God is revealed to us is full of characters as well. Today's story is no different. Samuel, the now elderly priest and judge has enjoyed the exhilaration of calling and appointing Saul as Israel's first king. He has railed against God after God condemns Saul's decision not to do all that God has instructed him to do. As I mentioned earlier, Samuel is

---

[17] 1 Samuel 9:2, New Revised Standard Version
[18] 1 Samuel 15: 10, NRSV

now grieving and heartbroken when we meet him today, and yet, God still has work for him to do. God has chosen a new king, and Samuel must now do God's work of anointing, setting apart this one. Samuel resists at first, fearing that Saul will accuse him of treason, but eventually he goes and seeks out Jesse's sons in Bethlehem. Saul and Samuel's falling out is widely known, so all of Bethlehem trembles over Samuel's arrival. As Eugene Peterson says, "Fierce and famous Samuel...wasn't known for his casual, drop-in visits. His enormous reputation didn't rest on a lifetime of accumulated small talk."[19] Samuel's arrival seems like trouble, but he calms their fears and invites them to a worship celebration, setting his sights on Jesse's sons.

As the sons arrive, Samuel looks each one over, an ancient beauty pageant of sorts. Samuel has a set idea of what a king should look like. He's only seen one king and that one was tall and handsome, so the next one will probably fit that mold, too. Eliab must look something like Saul 2.0 in Samuel's eyes, but God is quick to tell Samuel that God has a different plan in mind. God has tried the tall and handsome choice, the obvious, movie-star option before. God is less concerned with the external trappings and more focused on the heart of this next king. Like the scene in Cinderella where we watch young woman after young woman try to squeeze into the glass slipper, Jesse quickly runs out of sons. Samuel gets a bit nervous, "Are all your sons here?" Jesse then remembers David, the youngest who is off tending sheep. David is almost an afterthought. The Hebrew word translated here as the youngest "carries undertones of insignificance, of not counting for very much—certainly not a prime candidate for prestigious work. [In other words, David is] the family runt."[20] Samuel is not fazed by David's being the youngest, the overlooked, or the afterthought. Things can't go any further without him there, so everything grinds to a halt while they wait on him to come in from tending the sheep. I'm

---

[19] Eugene Peterson, *Leap Over a Wall*, 14.
[20] Peterson, 16.

guessing no one has ever waited on David for anything. As the youngest and as the one sent to tend the sheep, David has lived all of his young life on the fringes, far from the center of things, far from the limelight. God has not overlooked him, however. We don't know what exactly God sees in David's heart, but something points toward the heart of a king, the king of God's own choosing. While the narrator points out that David is good looking, he clearly does not look the part. He is not the one that any human director would cast in the role of king, but in God's eyes the part was written only for him. David is exactly the one to play the role God has in mind.

We are told more about David than about any other person in scripture.[21] The scribes who recorded his story for generations to come do not sanitize or gloss over his failings or his flaws. As the story unfolds, David will challenge any ideal we may hold of God's perfect king. To say that David is quite a character is an understatement. David is not simply quirky. He will prove himself to be impulsive, lustful, and arrogant. He will conquer giants and dance wildly. He will grasp greedily after power and people. He will grieve, he will rejoice, and he will scheme. And he will come to be known not as an afterthought, but as the great king of Israel and as the ancestor of the greatest king, the Son of David, Jesus the Christ. This brash nobody of a shepherd will begin to pave the way for the redeemer of the world. He is broken; he is sinful; and yet, the God of the universe is at work in and through him still. In David, in this one whom God sets apart as king of Israel, we see how the God of the universe is at work in and among the people of God, inviting and expecting characters of all kinds to do the work of God's kingdom.

The more time I spend in church, the more I treasure the characters I meet along the way. These characters have shaped and continue to

---

[21] Eugene Peterson, *Leap Over a Wall: Earthy Spirituality for Everyday Christians*, p. 3. Peterson points out (p. 24) that David's name is mentioned 600 times in the Hebrew Scriptures and 60 times in the New Testament.

shape not only who I am but how and where I see the kingdom of God.

I can still picture John Miller, a frail but mighty man who never missed a service or a bible study and almost never took no for an answer.[22] He had strong opinions on any number of issues, and he never hesitated to share them with anyone he could corner. He also never failed to surprise me. Every time I preached a sermon that I was just sure he would fervently disagree with, he would move his way through the line at the close of the service and share with me an insight he'd had (one that I hadn't intended) and thank me.

One impeccably dressed little lady named Frances shook my hand after worship the first Sunday I arrived and pronounced, "You're not bad for a lady preacher."

Walter was the custodian at one church. He had worked there since he was a teenager. He couldn't drive or live alone, so his sisters dropped him off and picked him up during the week and on Sundays. He spent most of his time hanging out on a pew in the narthex, but he welcomed every person to the church with a glowing smile and he knew where every last random item could be found.

Miss Joan rocked countless restless babies and toddlers including me to sleep in the church nursery. I'm not sure her voice ever rose above a whisper. I have never been so grateful to hand my own fussy and exhausted toddler over to another soul.

Marvin was a church treasurer who was not swayed by my charms or my preaching. In fact, I'm not sure he liked much about me at all. One day, I received a phone call in the church office. Marvin had traveled to Washington, DC to speak at a service for a man whom he had met only once, a man who spent his childhood summers in the small town where Marvin lived and worked. This man had given a bell to the

---

[22] Names have been changed.

church in gratitude for those summers. Marvin wanted to make sure the man's family knew how much he valued that bell as it rang on the hour. The phone call was from the man's widow. She was deeply touched by Marvin's words and his presence at the service. Would I please let him know how much that meant? The smile that crept on Marvin's face that Sunday morning when I shared the message with him was priceless.

There's Mr. Bates, my church basketball coach who would smoke a cigarette before practice and then encourage me to get angry early on in the game because he was sure it made me play better. Then there are the gossiping church ladies who showed up to help with my wedding armed with safety pins, hairspray, and extra pantyhose. My list could go on and on, and I'm guessing yours does too, or I hope it does.

When I think about the characters that God sets apart for the work of God's kingdom, I cannot help but marvel and give thanks. Because these characters—Marvin, Walter, Miss Joan, Frances, Samuel, and King David himself remind me in a deep and vivid way of the very character of God himself, the nature of the God whom we worship and serve. All of these people are characters in God's divine narrative. This God does not choose only the perfect or the pretty or the polished. This God does not dismiss the little ones or the awkward ones or the brash ones or the broken ones. This God seeks out the misfits, the outcasts, the scornful, the forgotten, the exuberant, and the fickle and uses us, all of us for the work of God's kingdom. God puts no one out to pasture. God puts no one in a corner. Every character has a part to play. Every person has role in this story.

This is our story, and this is God's story. Characters welcome.

Thanks be to God. Amen.

Mind the Gap
2 Samuel 11 and 12 and Psalm 51

October 21, 2018

At the close of last week's text, Joshua calls the people of Israel to remember who they are by faithfully worshipping the God who acts again and again to redeem them. Joshua challenges the people's claim that they will follow God. They insist that they can and will…but they don't, not consistently it seems. Following Joshua's death, Israel cries out for a new leader, so God raises up judges to lead them and protect them. God takes pity on them as they face persecution and oppression:

> But whenever the judge die[s], they…relapse and behave worse than their ancestors, following other gods…They [do] not drop any of their practices or their stubborn ways.[23]

The book of Judges tells stories of some of our favorite biblical superheroes, like Deborah and Samson, but the book is more than its stories. The narrative recounts a dark and chaotic time when the descendants of Jacob's sons fight one another as well as other nations. The book of Judges ends on a somber note: "In those days there was no king in Israel; all the people did what was right in their own eyes."[24] Hope comes when Hannah's child Samuel is called to serve God and the people, but when an aging Samuel appoints his own corrupt sons as judges, the people have had enough. They come to Samuel and ask for "a king…like other nations."[25] God tells Samuel to listen to their voice, while warning them about what life with a king looks like. Speaking God's words, Samuel emphasizes to Israel that life with a king will be filled with give and take: the people will be expected to

---

[23] Judges 2: 19, New Revised Standard Version
[24] Judges 21: 25, NRSV
[25] 1 Samuel 8: 5, NRSV

give, and the king will take anything and everything that he wants. In his description of a king, Samuel uses the word *take* 6 times in 8 verses.[26] The people are not dissuaded; they still want a king. So a king is what they get. Saul is the first king; David is the second.

More is written about David than any other person in the Hebrew Scriptures. He is the handsome shepherd boy who has a special grasp on God's heart. He is the greatest king Israel has ever known. He is a fierce warrior and a passionate leader. He unites the people and brings the Ark of the Covenant to Jerusalem. God makes a covenant with David and promises to build a dynasty through him. The first time the prophet Nathan is sent to David, he comes to announce that dynasty. Nathan now arrives with a promise of a different kind. David has maneuvered to cover his tracks following his affair with Bathsheba. He has schemed to have her husband Uriah killed in battle, a battle that David has opted to sit out. God is not happy. Nathan is not showing up with great, good news this time. Nathan is charged with breaking this news to David. He has not come to tell David he has won the Powerball lottery. No, Nathan must tell David the hard truth.

David's sordid tale is compelling in a way, but such sordid tales have all but lost their shock value these days. Sadly we're are no longer surprised when we hear stories of people in power behaving badly. So David's taking Bathsheba and his taking Uriah's life is not terribly surprising in 2018. We shake our heads, but we have almost come to expect powerful people to do such things. God has warned us after all. Kings take. It is what they do. The bar is not set all that high. Perhaps the most shocking piece of the story is what David does next. He repents.

In bible study on Wednesday, we tried to come up with a prominent person who had fallen from grace and then repented, genuinely

---

[26] See 1 Samuel 8: 11-19, NRSV

repented. We could not come up with one. We also wondered how we as a society might respond if it actually happened. It is so rare, I'm not sure we would know what to do. We have grown so accustomed to public figures fessing up only when they get caught, then covering their tracks, and spinning their words. How would we respond to a genuine confession? Would we be impressed? Would we see it as a sign of weakness? Would we even be able to trust that it was true?

Repentance is not a word we use very often, especially in the larger world. True confessions are associated with the latest celebrity scandal or the dark carved wood doors of confessional booths in the Roman Catholic churches we see in the movies, or for some of us, in our memories. A few years ago, Pope Francis broke with protocol in the midst of a worship service. It was during Lent, and he was supposed to finish his sermon and head straight to an empty confessional booth to hear confession from "the ordinary faithful," as one account read. Instead, he headed directly to an already occupied booth and knelt in full view of everyone, confessing his own sins first. In watching one video of the moment, you can hear the whispers of those immediately around him.[27] It's disruptive and humbling and refreshing and rare. With the scandals currently gripping the church, one wonders if we'll see a sight like that again any time soon. Because not only is such a move rare, it is also disruptive. It is not what we do. The Catholic Church's troubles are high profile, but they are not unique. Churches across the spectrum have fallen short repeatedly in how we have treated children, women, immigrants, members of the LGBTQ+ community, and people of color. There is much to confess. And yet we dodge, we get defensive, we make excuses, or we just ignore it and hope it will go away.

So what David does here is almost foreign; the words he offers in response to God's word spoken through Nathan is utterly

---

[27] https://youtu.be/BKHKmEtpWao

unfamiliar…Except we do it every week. We gather in this place and confess our sin, the ways we have broken the covenant individually and as a community. It is an odd but holy practice, not one that we learn anywhere else. But then again, we are an odd and holy tribe. We do not play by the rules of the larger world—or at least we're not supposed to—and for all of his flaws, David does not either.

You may have been surprised to hear Andy's voice in the middle of the second lesson. If you followed along in the pew bible you may have noticed the header to Psalm 51 where it points to David's conversation with Nathan as the prompt for the writing of the psalm. One scholar observes that, "In many medieval manuscripts…a gap was left by copyists to allow for the reading of Psalm 51."[28] It makes sense, doesn't it? If we read David's confession in 2 Samuel without that gap, without Psalm 51, the words ring dangerously hollow, the confession seems too easy, too pat, too much like the easy confessions we hear all too often, too much like the ones I for one am tempted to offer myself. Maybe I need that pause, that gap, too. Maybe we all do. Maybe that is one role this hour on Sunday morning can serve. Maybe this can be our gap, our pause when we encounter the word of God ourselves and recognize how needed our confession is.

Confession and repentance are not our default drive, after all. They have to be learned. And who are going to teach us? Through the ages, the gathered community has practiced confession and repentance, but I'm pretty sure practice has yet to make us perfect. I'm not sure perfection should even be our aim, but I do think we could be better, that I could do better. Confession is good for the soul; it is often said. And for individuals it is true, but could it be good for the collective

---

[28] Bruce Birch, "The First and Second Books of Samuel," *The New Interpreter's Bible*, vol. II, 1295.

soul as well? Could the church's teaching somehow begin to shape or re-shape the larger world? Maybe.

I am not suggesting that we move through the world apologetically. We are called to be bold in sharing the love of Christ, bold in working for justice, bold in making room for voices of those others would dismiss or overlook. But I wonder what it would look like for us to be bold in our willingness to admit when we have wronged God and one another, not only in here each week but in our daily comings and goings. Our tradition embraces David as this great king, and we take solace in his being human like us, a man with feet of clay through whom God builds an earthly dynasty and brings us the greatest king of all in Jesus Christ. But what if we embraced David's boldness in confessing his sins, in his pleading with God to create in him a clean heart, to restore his spirit and make him whole? David, Israel's great and glorious king is a child of the covenant, as are we. We say it every week: we are a covenant people. We are bound to God and to one another through the work of our promise-making and promise-keeping God. This God makes a covenant with us and calls us to love God and neighbor. It is that simple and that hard. We are often tempted to speak of God's forgiveness and love in Jesus Christ, but we meet that love here, too. David is bold to repent because he knows the God of the universe to be a God of unfailing love. "Have mercy, O God, *according to your steadfast love*," the psalm begins. In God we meet mercy grounded in steadfast love and forgiveness founded on faithfulness. God's faithfulness and mercy carve a gap of a different sort, a holy space for our confession to be heard. Without that gap, we might begin to believe that we do something to earn that mercy and forgiveness, that by speaking just the right words, we will get a hearing. But God is poised to hear us well before we speak. God's mercy is the starting point. God's love shapes a space for coming clean. For David and for us.

David's sin is horrendous. His arrogance is appalling. He is not what I would call a "model citizen." And yet, if we are to be true to our calling to share God's good news with the world in word and deed, David might just be a model we could follow. Not in his scheming and dodging. We're far too good at that as a society already. What if we carried David's trust of God's unfailing love and his bold confessing with us out into God's world? Can you imagine a world where humility and confession were the norm? Where genuine repentance was routine? Me neither. But I would like to try.

In the name of the Father and of the Son and of the Holy Spirit. Amen.

If Only…
2 Kings 5:1-14

November 4, 2018

This morning's text finds us in a divided kingdom. The golden era of Solomon's reign is now a long-ago dream. Israel is the kingdom to the north; Judah lies to the south. They are now enemy states at peace for the moment, with other enemies on every side. We are also now in the time when prophets rise up not to gaze on crystal balls and speculate about the future, but to speak God's truth into the current moment, a truth those in power often do not want to hear. Moments ago we met Elisha, the successor to one of Israel's most famous prophets, Elijah. The story of Naaman's healing is part of a larger collection of accounts of Elisha's power as a healer, a man of God. And this episode at least reads like a script for a play on a stage.

Naaman appears in verse 1 and is described as a commander in the king of Syria's army, a great warrior who has known victory and success on the battlefield. And yet, he has leprosy, or some kind of skin condition that is uncomfortable and likely unsightly. Clearly, he wants to be healed. The next voice we hear is one of an unnamed slave girl, a captive from Israel. Then there are the kings of Aram and Israel. And finally there are more servants, or slaves as the Hebrew reads, who complete the cast. While we are given much more detail about Naaman and the king of Israel's melodramatic and almost comic response to Naaman's request, I find myself wanting to know more about the slave girl. She has no name; she has no earthly power, and yet without her words, we have no story, and Naaman still has leprosy. With the one phrase, "If only…" his healing begins. Even in the midst of captivity and oppression, this unnamed, unknown girl points the way to the one true God and to the source of her captor's healing. Because you know Naaman has tried everything else. A man such as him has access to every trick in the book, every snake oil imaginable. I imagine that he has tried it all, and still he suffers. And one could rightly imagine that this girl who has been forcibly taken from her home and her family might actually savor his suffering. Instead, she offers a word of hope, THE word of hope and healing that Naaman has needed all along.

It takes him a bit of time to get there of course. He does not go straight to the man of God but to his king, who in turn sends him to the king of Israel. Even the king of Israel, the one who should know what is going on, misses the message at first. He thinks the Syrian king is trying to pick a fight, seeking to set him up and undo their tenuous truce. Only when the king tears his clothes and makes a spectacle does Elisha catch wind of the drama and ask that Naaman be sent to him. Then Elisha does not even bother to leave his tent. He sends out simple instructions, and now it is Naaman's turn to lose it. In his tantrum he almost walks away from his one true chance to be healed. He thinks he is worthy of a grand show, and he is put out with the suggestion that he will find healing in the muddy waters of the pitiful Jordan. Again, it is the voice of unknown slaves who draw him back. It is the whispers of unnamed and overlooked people, the more-than-ordinary ones who convince him that the prophet's plan is worth a shot.

This morning we are celebrating All Saints' Sunday when we give thanks for our dear ones who have died this past year. It is also a time when we pause and give thanks for the ones who have come before us in faith and the ones who share the journey with us now, the ones who have pointed us back to the one true God, the ones who have told us and shown us what it is to be faithful, whether we know their names or not.

As Jay Slagle returned from covering a high school cross country race in McCool Junction, Nebraska, he could not shake one question, "Who was that kid in last place?" After delving a bit he learned the story of Noah Lambrecht, a child who was adopted from the hospital after he had been abandoned and left behind because his birth parents were no doubt overwhelmed and overmatched by his staggering health problems. He was born with a host of issues, not the least of which was that the vessels to his heart were not connected correctly. After multiple surgeries, Noah's new parents were permitted to take him home. Doctors did not expect him to survive until his first birthday. But survive he did, and in the spring of seventh grade he said he wanted to run cross country in the fall. His parents, Gaylord and Sheri thought he'd get over that idea over the summer, but he didn't, and come fall he laced up alongside his classmates. In middle school the races were only a mile long, so his coming in a few minutes behind the other runners didn't get much notice. When he laced up for the high school team, things were different, and people began to worry. Noah had never run three miles before. He had a pacemaker. He would be last or almost last at every meet. But then, Slagle writes:

> Just before Noah's first high school meet, the upperclassmen approached Coach Underwood with a question. 'After we finish our race, can we go back and run with Noah? He could use our help.' Coach Underwood responded that they could run with Noah as long as they didn't give him a competitive advantage over a nearby runner. At that first meet in Superior, a handful of teammates joined Noah to run his last 800 meters. Not cheering, not giving sympathy. Just running with a new member of their family.[29]

Noah still finishes eight to ten minutes behind everyone else, and his teammates, even ones who have now headed to college still encourage him and run alongside when they come home to visit. But here's the piece that floors me: runners from other schools run alongside him, too. Slagle writes:

---

[29] https://ovalsandtrails.com/blog/2018/10/19/the-runner-with-the-broken-heart

For a boy who finishes last more often than not, it was impossible for Noah to fit all of his cross-country highlights into a fifty-minute phone interview. A few stand out. At Hebron's meet, the football players practice in the morning so they can cheer on their home team in the afternoon. McCool Junction runs that meet every year. At this year's meet, two Hebron football players wearing blue jeans and boots were the first to join Noah. Then his teammates, then runners from other schools. By the finish line, there were 75 to 80 runners with him. It's always just kids, and never adults. The adults are too busy crying.[30]

Noah is amazing and inspiring, but I am inspired by these unnamed students, too. They stand to gain nothing from running alongside Noah. And yet, these students, these children, like that slave girl come alongside anyway.

One of you pointed out this past week that the reference to Elisha's story taking place in a divided nation struck a chord, because we are, too. And yet, lest we forget, we are also children of the covenant, children of God. *That* is our most fundamental and essential identity. Like the slave girl in Naaman's household we too know where the healer lives, we know with whom the healing lies. Someone somewhere pointed the way for us. Someone somewhere raced alongside us when we were panting for breath. Someone somewhere gave us hope for tomorrow when the way ahead seemed dark and foreboding. Someone, somewhere whispered, "If only…" Someone, somewhere, dared to suggest that we give faith a try. Like the slave girl and the slaves along for the ride, like the football players in cowboy boots from a rival team, those someones stood to gain nothing for showing us the way. There was nothing in it for them, and yet because of their

---

[30] https://ovalsandtrails.com/blog/2018/10/19/the-runner-with-the-broken-heart

testimony, because of their witness we, too, have found ourselves being healed.

We will close worship singing one of my mother's favorite hymns, "I Sing a Song of the Saints of God." To some the lyrics about meeting other saints "in shops or at tea" are a bit silly or trivial, but I find hope there. Because I am not Elisha or Paul or Peter. I am not Mother Teresa or Martin Luther King, Jr. or Mr. Rogers. And heaven knows, I am not Jesus. Not even close. But in the whisper of an unknown slave girl I am reminded that I, too, know the one who alone can bring healing, so I too can be a saint for someone. We need saints everywhere all the time, but in a divided kingdom, we need them desperately. I do not own a halo, but I do own running shoes and a couple of pairs of cowboy boots. Maybe it's my turn to put them on, to follow the children's lead, to run alongside a stranger or a member of the opposing team and offer a word of healing, too. "If only…"

In the name of the Father and of the Son and of the Holy Spirit. Amen.

Each Other's Angels
Job 3, 5, and 7, selected verses

August 14, 2016

And just like that, our short three-act play lands us in the thick of Job's grief. As I mentioned last week, the book of Job is not a blueprint of why we suffer or how to grieve or how to walk alongside someone who is grieving. Instead it more of a snapshot or a quickly evolving portrait of the *what now* part of suffering. And what a portrait we get. Unlike a Google map, we are not given the option of pulling back and getting a view from a distance. Instead we are brought face-to-face with Job's open wounds and raw suffering. There is no buffer, no filter. We sit with his three friends and watch and listen as this man, once considered the greatest, most blessed of men wrestles out loud with his agony and loss.

Job's friends are often criticized and dismissed. After doing the good and faithful work of showing up and sitting silently with their friend, they open their mouths. In their defense, it cannot be easy to sit in silence alongside Job. His losses are incomprehensible. His suffering has rendered him almost unrecognizable. He is covered in ashes and boils. He is frail, and he is broken, with shaved head and tattered clothes. The friends wail at the sight of him. Then they tear their own clothes and drench themselves in ashes. And they sit with him for a full week in silence.

Job is the first to speak. He utters a scathing and bitter soliloquy, cursing the day he was born, cursing his birthday. Each time his birthday rolled around my grandfather would make a joke about having another year piled on top of a tall stack of years was better than the alternative. In this moment, Job could not disagree more. His birthday has become a cause for despair rather than celebration. His language speaks of undoing creation. Where God has called forth light, Job calls for darkness. Where God has called forth life, Job cries out for death. Despair has engulfed him. Anger and grief have all but swallowed him up.

Job pauses, and Eliphaz speaks. We hear only a portion of Eliphaz's speech, but even in that snippet, we hear enough. Eliphaz along with the other two friends offers suggestions for how Job can make sense of all that he is enduring. Eliphaz raises questions about whether Job has actually lived such a sin-free life as he claims. Innocents do not suffer, Eliphaz insists. Later on in his speech, Eliphaz will go on to say that Job is arrogantly resisting God's corrections, God's discipline. He suggests that all will balance out in the end, that this, too, shall pass. I can almost hear the "tsk, tsk" and see the sanctimonious expression on his dusty face as he tries to explain things to Job and maybe comfort himself along the way.

A few years ago, I read an article by a pastor named Christian Piatt entitled, "Ten Clichés Christians Should Never Use." Among those ten things is: "Everything happens for a reason." He explains:

> I've heard this said more times than I care to. I'm not sure where it came from either, but it's definitely not in the Bible. The closest thing I can come up with is 'To everything, there is a season,' but that's not exactly the same. The fact is that faith, by definition, is not reasonable. If it could be empirically verified with facts or by using the scientific method, it wouldn't be faith. It would be a theory. Also, consider how such a pithy phrase sounds to someone who was [sexually assaulted]. Do you really mean to tell them there's a reason that happened? Better to be quiet, listen and if appropriate, mourn alongside

them. But don't dismiss grief or tragedy with such a meaningless phrase.[31]

I sympathize with Piatt's passion, but I sympathize with Eliphaz, too, because I want there to be a reason; we want there to be a reason. Eliphaz wants there to be a reason for Job's trials. So does Job. And yet, we and the original hearers know that there really is no justifiable reason for his suffering other than a wager between God and his appointed adversary, a narrative set-up drawn from an ancient folktale. We really do not get a reason. As we discussed last week, the story of Job is less concerned with *why* of suffering than with the *what now*. Eliphaz would rather focus on the why, because the *what now* is, too, hard to face. There are no words for the *what now*, and that is exactly what Eliphaz can't stomach. The story of Job does not answer the *why*, but it does place the *what now* right in front of us in all of its ugliness and messiness, all of its raw suffering and open wounds. We can't dodge it, try as we may.

Job responds to Elipahz and then turns his words to God. He wrestles out loud with his misery and with God, doing his thinking about God "at the top of his lungs, directing his shouts to God's face."[32] And to their credit, the friends stick around, even while Job screams at God. This is not a polite conversation or a carefully crafted liturgy:

> I will not keep silent.
> In the agony of my spirit, I will speak;
> In the bitterness of my soul, I will complain.[33]

Job goes on to rail against God, mocking the beautiful words of Psalm 8 that we heard earlier this morning. The psalmist's awe-filled poetry

---

[31] https://sojo.net/articles/christian-cliches/ten-cliches-christians-should-never-use

[32] Ellen F. Davis, *Getting Involved with God: Rediscovering the Old Testament* (New York: Cowley, 2001), 130.

[33] Job 7: 11, The Voice Bible

becomes spiteful bile in Job's mouth. He is fed up with God and with the ways his life has been utterly destroyed.

Job's tirade is uncomfortable to watch, and his words are painful to hear, but my sense is that for many they may actually elicit a sigh of relief. While the first two chapters of Job may be drawn from an ancient folktale, the writers of Job's story are inspired by the experience of the many Jobs in their midst, the Israelites whose lives have been utterly destroyed by the fall of Jerusalem and the exile to Babylon. My hunch is that the story rings true for many of us as well. We know Job; maybe we have been Job. When lives are shredded because of a pink slip, a child's diagnosis, a spouse's betrayal, a cataclysmic event on any scale, we are Job, and we too want to rail against God. The gift of Job is that it is sacred scripture, holy words that do not sugar coat despair or shy away from the fiercest of agony or suffering. The sacred text that gives us the grandeur of creation, the wonder of the burning bush, and the abundance of manna in the wilderness is the very same sacred text that gives us the gut-wrenching despair of a good man, a man who loses all that he loves for no good reason, a man who lashes out at God in anger and anguish. These are holy words, and Job's rage is a holy rage. God can take all that Job hurls at him. God is fine, and really, so is Job. It is Job's friends who struggle with what to do, what to say, what to make of it all.

Job has friends; Job needs angels. I am not thinking of biblical angels like Gabriel or the ones who sing from the heavens on Christmas Eve. No, I'm thinking of flesh and blood angels like the ones who showed up in Orlando earlier this summer on the heels of the senseless ambush at Pulse nightclub. You are no doubt familiar with the Westboro folks who insist on showing up to harass and antagonize mourners in the name of God—no God I worship by the way. Since they began these protests years ago, they have been greeted by faithful angels who place themselves between the mourners and those who seethe with vitriol and hurl hate-filled words. These angels have been ordinary church types ranging in ages and backgrounds; they have been bikers in leather and bandanas; and in June they were actually dressed as angels, sporting white robes with sleeves attached to dowels so that when raised they resemble oversized angel wings.[34] Time and again, these angels shield the mourners from the protests, but that is not all. They also show up in the midst of the ugliness and pain and create a space for grieving. The do not edit, correct, or filter the grieving. The do not try to fix the grief, nor do they preach to the grieving either. They do not fumble with clichés. They do not try to explain. They simply and powerfully hold space for the grief and the grieving.

A singer from North Carolina, David Lamotte sings a song entitled, "We Are Each Other's Angels.":

> Go answer your calling
> Go and fill somebody's cup
> And if you see an angel falling
> Won't you stop and help them up
>
> 'Cause we are each other's angels
> And we meet when it is time
> We keep each other going
> And we show each other signs
>
> Sometimes you will stumble
> Sometimes you might fall down
> Sometimes you will get lonely
> With all these people around
> You might shiver when the wind blows
> And you might get blown away

---

[34] http://www.npr.org/sections/thetwo-way/2016/06/19/482698337/angels-from-orlandos-theater-community-guard-mourners-from-protesters

You might even lose your colors
But don't you ever lose your faith.[35]

Angels do not shy away from the grieving. They do not run from or try to numb the pain. They do not insist on explaining or on giving pat answers to soothe their own discomfort. Instead, they show up, they stand up, they lift up, and they spread their wings to shelter the hurting and the grieving, the angry and the broken. We are each other's angels, church. For those who are grieving, angry or hurting, we are saving a space for you. For those called to be angels here and now, it's time to spread our wings.

In the name of the Father and of the Son and of the Holy Spirit. Amen.

---

[35] http://www.allthelyrics.com/lyrics/david_lamotte/we_are_each_others_angels-lyrics-1250482.html#ixzz4HEmC568m. A video of David singing this song can be found here: https://youtu.be/U8H0wbdxbAM

And So I Kept Living
Job 14 and 19

August 21, 2016

In the chapters between last week's text and today's, Job has had further discussions with his friends, or "miserable comforters," as he comes to call them.[36] They have continued to insist that Job must be guilty, wicked, and/or ungrateful because only the guilty, wicked, and ungrateful suffer. Job argues back insisting that their claims don't hold water, that human experience and suffering are not that neat and tidy. Before his suffering began, he might have agreed with the "miserable comforters." His experience of both his struggles and their unhelpful explanations has changed his mind and his heart. In last week's text, we heard Job insist that he was ready to die, to be done with his miserable existence. Now something seems to be shifting, not dramatically, but it's a shift nonetheless. [Read Job 14:7-15; 19:23-27]

In the first part of today's text, we hear Job insisting that there is hope for a tree even if there is no hope for him. By design trees are built to regenerate. If you have ever tried to get rid of a locust tree or a wisteria vine, you have caught a glimpse of this tenacity. There is a determination, a stubborn insistence on survival. Even a whiff of water is enough to bring it back to life. Human beings are not built the same way, Job thinks. In a creative turn, he wonders aloud if God could just hide him in the shadowy world of Sheol until God gets over his wrath. Job seems to think God might just grow homesick for him, longing for the one God shaped from the dust. Job finds himself in the thick of the unimaginable, a moment "when it feels easier to just swim down" as the song from *Hamilton* says.[37] And yet, somehow, Job begins to imagine a way forward. While he may not quite recognize it, like a tree

---

36 Job 16: 2, NRSV
37 "It's Quiet Uptown" https://www.youtube.com/watch?v=F8rlHxyzJyA

he has caught a whiff of something that resembles water, and maybe it's enough to turn the corner.

As we move into the second part of the today's reading, we hear Job's imagination gain traction. We hear him moving toward something that begins to resemble hope. The Hebrew in Job is some of the most complex and confusing language in all of scripture. This portion of chapter 19 has confounded even the wisest of scholars. We hear the word redeemer and immediately certain images spring to mind. Maybe you see Cristo Redentor, the statue of Christ standing watch over Rio. Maybe you hear strains of Handel's *Messiah*. Maybe you hum a familiar hymn. Clearly the notion of a redeemer has captured our collective religious imagination. We hear redeemer and we think of Jesus, but as one scholar points out, the word "*redeemer* was a human word before it was a theological word."[38] The word *goel* speaks of family obligations. The *goel* is a "kinsman-defender":

> [A family member who] would buy back family property sold in distress, recover what had been stolen, redeem a kinsman sold into slavery, or avenge a murdered kinsman's blood.[39]

In the midst of his suffering, having lost his children, his health, his fortune, and his future for no good reason, Job imagines his redeemer, his champion, someone who will stand with him, someone who will help him recover, regain his footing. Scholars debate whether this redeemer is God or a human vindicator who will stand with Job as he faces God. Maybe it's one or the other. Maybe it's a mixture of all of the above. Bottom line, Job is able to imagine an ally, a witness, a redeemer, and because of that redeemer, Job is able to imagine a future, a next chapter, a next breath. Job is made of strong stuff. It's not so

---

[38] Rolf Jacobson, "I Love to Tell The Story" podcast #229:
http://www.workingpreacher.org/narrative_podcast.aspx?podcast_id=765
[39] Carol A. Newsom, "The Book of Job," The New Interpreter's Bible, Vol. IV, (Nashville: Abingdon, 1996) 478.

much that he has won some genetic lottery that gives him a built-in predisposition to optimism. It's deeper than that. He has been shaped and nurtured in a tradition that understands and experiences redemption, salvation, and justice in the midst of turmoil, despair, and failure. He is convinced that he will meet his redeemer—human or divine because at his core he knows that his story is not over and that all of this is not for naught. That is the community that has shaped him; that is the community that has saved his story, maybe not in stone, but on pages that have survived the ages.

Trapped in exile, the people of Israel have every reason to give up, to lose hope, and to stop looking for redemption, but they have not been built that way. They have been shaped as a covenant community, a people whose God has shown up for them time and again, one whose God has sent leaders like Abraham and Sarah, Moses and Miriam who march them toward God's promise. They have known redemption, and they have learned to stubbornly trust that they will see it again, even when all is lost. This is the community that has nurtured Job. It's not a matter of easy answers or simplistic theology. It is matter of a God who stays faithful, a God who redeems, and a community who counts on, expects, and even pushes God to redeem again, even when everything around them tells them that redemption is unimaginable, when the larger world insists that their redeemer is nothing more than a pipe dream.

This morning we sit on the cusp of a new school year when students of all ages will once again learn and study and explore new ideas and have their horizons stretched and their minds challenged. Last week I insisted that we are each other's angels, but we are each other's teachers, too. We want the best for our children, for all children really. We want them to grow to be strong and wise and kind and brave. We also want them to know that they are loved, treasured, that they are not alone, no matter what. That sounds so simple, but it is ever so crucial. Depression among youth and young adults is on the rise. A recent study tells us:

> More than 40 percent of [gay, lesbian, bisexual and transgender] students reported that they had seriously considered suicide, and 29 percent had made attempts to do so in the year before they took the survey.[40]

Other studies tell us that suicide has reached a 30-year high. Who or what can turn that tide? How will those without hope find hope? How will they know that their redeemer lives?

The non-profit group To Write Love on Her Arms is trying to help them do just that. It began with a story:

> When Jamie met Renee…she was struggling with addiction, depression, self-injury, and suicidal thoughts. He wrote about the five days he spent with her before she entered a treatment center, and he sold T-shirts to help cover the cost.[41]

Jamie's story continues in his own words:

> She has known such great pain; haunted dreams as a child, the near-constant presence of evil ever since. She has felt the [unwelcome] touch of awful…men, battled depression and addiction, and attempted suicide. Her arms remember razor blades, fifty scars that speak of self-inflicted wounds… She is full of contrast, more alive and closer to death than anyone I've known, like a Johnny Cash song or some theatre star. She owns attitude and humor beyond her 19 years, and when she tells me her story, she is humble and quiet and kind, shaped by the pain

---

[40] http://www.nytimes.com/2016/08/12/health/gay-lesbian-teenagers-violence.html?_r=0
[41] https://twloha.com/learn/

of a hundred lifetimes. I sit privileged but breaking as she shares. Her life has been so dark yet there is some soft hope in her words. [The local hospital will not or cannot admit her, and she must wait five days before she can be admitted to rehab. So Jamie and others wait with her.]

Sunday night is church, and many gather after the service to pray for Renee, this her last night before entering rehab. Some are strangers but all are friends tonight. The prayers move from broken to bold, all encouraging. We're talking to God, but I think as much, we're talking to her, telling her she's loved, saying she does not go alone…After church our house fills with friends, there for a few more moments before goodbye. Everyone has some gift for her, some note or hug or piece of encouragement. She pulls me aside and tells me she would like to give me something. I smile surprised, wondering what it could be. We walk through the crowded living room, to the garage and her stuff. She hands me her last razor blade… As we arrive at the treatment center, she finishes: 'The stars are always there but we miss them in the dirt and clouds. We miss them in the storms. Tell them to remember hope. We have hope.'

I have watched life come back to her, and it has been a privilege. When our time with her began, someone suggested [taking] shifts but that is the language of business. Love is something better. I have been challenged and changed, reminded that love is that simple answer to so many of our hardest questions. Don Miller says we're called to hold our hands against the wounds of a broken world, to stop the bleeding.[42]

---

[42] https://twloha.com/learn/story/

Born out of this story, To Write Love on Her Arms claims a bold vision:

> You were created to love and be loved. You were meant to live life in relationship with other people, to know and be known. You need to know your story is important, and you're part of a bigger story. You need to know your life matters…We live in a difficult world, a broken world. We believe everyone can relate to pain, all of us live with questions, and all of us get stuck in moments. You need to know you're not alone in the places you feel stuck.[43]

Jamie and his friends did not preach at Renee. They did not tell her that her thoughts or behaviors were an affront to God. They did not tell her to change in order for God to love her. Instead they walked alongside her and showed her love and compassion, just as God had showed them. Each year, To Write Love on Her Arms encourages people to observe Suicide Prevention Day on September 10, to take a public stand in the name of life and hope. For their theme this year, they have chosen: "And so I kept living." It sounds like a theme Job could have written.

Even when his friends failed him. Even when the world crumbled around him. Even when he longed for death, longed to be hidden from God. Even when he was unimaginably stuck, somehow Job was able to see through the dirt and the clouds to the stars, to know that redemption was possible, and to insist that he wanted to see his redeemer face to face. He was not able to imagine such redemption on his own. It was not in his genetic makeup. It was deeper than that. Job knew hope because his community had taught him how to hope. He knew that redemption was possible because his community had known

---

[43] https://twloha.com/learn/vision/

redemption before and was stubbornly convinced that they would know it again, no matter what their captors said.

While scholars agree that there was probably no Job, no land of Uz, you and I know plenty of Jobs. We have walked alongside and prayed alongside and wept alongside Jobs who have lost everything, Jobs who have faced the unimaginable. Maybe you have faced the unimaginable. Maybe you have been Job. Maybe you are Job now. You have felt that holy rage; you have stared down the unimaginable, and yet you are here. You have managed to imagine a next step, a next chapter, a next breath.

As a church we boldly claim that we **know** that our Redeemer lives. We have met him in Jesus Christ. And we have met him because someone somewhere made sure we knew the stories, made sure we learned how to see the stars behind the dirt and the clouds, made sure we knew how to push our roots toward a whiff of water, to press through rocky soil and find the sun, made sure to teach us how to hope. If you are stuck, frightened, or afraid, hang on. Together we will wait for the clouds to pass. Together we will wait for the slightest whiff of water. Together we will look for our Redeemer. Together we will keep living.

In the name of God, our Rock and our Redeemer. Amen.

Waiting Room
Psalm 13

June 18, 2017

This week's psalm takes a dramatic turn from last week's and plunges us from joyous laughter into the depths of despair. Psalm 13: 1-4:

> How long, O LORD? Will you forget me forever?
>> How long will you hide your face from me?
> ² How long must I bear pain in my soul,
>> and have sorrow in my heart all day long?
> How long shall my enemy be exalted over me?
>
> ³ Consider and answer me, O LORD my God!
>> Give light to my eyes, or I will sleep the sleep of death,
> ⁴ and my enemy will say, "I have prevailed";
>> my foes will rejoice because I am shaken.

"How long, O Lord?" Rarely has a sentence captured so much in four small words. Uttered by the psalmist thousands of years ago, these same words echoed across the world over the past week.

> Congressmen come under attack while playing baseball.
> —how long, O Lord, will anger give way to violence?
> A high-rise apartment building is engulfed in flames in London.
> —how long, O Lord, will innocents suffer and die?
> Verdicts are returned that disappoint and divide us.
> —how long, O Lord, must we wait for justice for all?

This weekend marks the anniversary of that day two years ago when a gunman took the lives of people at bible study because of their race.

—how long, O Lord, will hatred and fear fill our news feeds and nation?

A destroyer collides with a cargo ship of the coast of Japan, and seven sailors are killed.

—how long, O Lord?

The question gets asked closer to home as well.

Symptoms crop up, tests are run.
—how long, O Lord, do I have to wait for answers?
A child struggles with addiction.
—how long, O Lord, until she finds her way through recovery?
A friend battles depression
—how long, O Lord, until the light shines for him again?
A spouse's health declines, hospice is brought in.
—how long, O Lord, do we have left?
A parent declines into the world of dementia.
—how long, O Lord?

The answers do not come. At least not right away. And so we wait.

The psalmist waits, too. His heart is heavy, and his voice is weary, and he cries out insisting that God turn his face to him, that God see him. The musical *Dear, Evan Hansen* opens with the lead character singing a song entitled "Waving through a Window." Evan is an outsider who longs to be seen, too:

On the outside, always looking in
Will I ever be more than I've always been?
'Cause I'm tap, tap, tapping on the glass

I'm waving through a window
I try to speak, but nobody can hear
So I wait around for an answer to appear
While I'm watch, watch, watching people pass
I'm waving through a window, oh
Can anybody see, is anybody waving back at me?[44]

The psalmist is tapping on the glass, too. While the world swirls around him, he feels forgotten and unnoticed except by enemies who seek his destruction. He is waiting for an answer from God, he is tired of waiting for this answer, and he is not afraid to tell God just how tired he is.

I feel like a broken record at times, but once again I find myself grateful for the honesty of the psalms. Too many of us have been told that certain conversations with God are off-limits, that we should not question God, should not get frustrated with God, should not get angry at God or impatient with God. And yet, here in sacred scripture, we hear the psalmist doing just that.

A few months ago I saw a video of an experiment in a waiting room at an eye doctor's office. It's a fairly typical waiting room, one with chairs lined up just a little too closely together against the wall and around a corner. There are magazines that no one really reads and some generic muzak playing on the speakers. A woman enters, signs in, and finds a seat. Moments later, a tone sounds, and everyone else in the waiting room stands up and sits back down. The woman looks around, amused and a bit uncomfortable, apparently wondering if she has missed the memo, if she has missed some instructions. Over the next few minutes, tones continue to sound, and people continue to stand on cue. And the woman joins them. She wants to wait the right way, whatever that may be. Slowly, the rest of the people waiting are called back for their

---

[44] https://genius.com/Benj-pasek-and-justin-paul-waving-through-a-window-lyrics

appointments. Even after she is the last person in the waiting room, she continues to stand when the tone sounds. Another person comes in to wait, and she shows him how it's done.[45]

It's a silly experiment. As I watched it, I found myself saying out loud that it was absurd and that I would never follow along, that I'd know better. But the reality is that we tend to conform to the setting in which we find ourselves. We look for clues and take cues from those around us. In this case the woman learned a new way to wait, a silly way to wait perhaps, but the community around her did in fact shape how she waited.

The community shapes how we wait, too. The larger culture has very little patience for waiting. In the larger world, we are trained to expect instant information and immediate responses and to demand them if we don't get the answers when we expect them. In church, somehow, it's different. In this place and with these people, our waiting is shaped, too. As we sing and pray and cry and listen and laugh and worship together, our expectations of the world and of ourselves of others and of God are shaped, too. Or at least they should be. But somehow, we get the sense that there is only one faithful way to wait—quietly and patiently and stoically with our hands folded in our laps and our mouths shut. I still have people apologize to me for crying in worship. I still have people apologize to me for questioning God. I still have people apologize to me for doubting or being angry or wondering what the point of all of this is. On my own, I do not have the answers, so I point back to the psalms, the community's ancient prayer book. Silent stoicism and stiff upper lips are not scriptural. Anger, doubt, sadness, and weeping are. And so we dive back into the psalms, to re-learn the cues, to sit and stand alongside each other, to be shaped once again and to learn what it means to wait faithfully. In holy scripture we are reminded that feeling forgotten, wondering and doubting and

---

[45] http://dailyoftheday.com/social-experiment-of-the-day-social-conformity/

questioning are not something to confess or apologize for. They are in fact part of that faithful waiting, too.

You may have noticed that I only read a part of the psalm. When we read the whole thing in one sitting it seems like a piece of the psalm is missing, because the last two verses seem to be so different from the first four. Psalm 13:5-6:

> But I trusted in your steadfast love;
>   my heart shall rejoice in your salvation.
> [6] I will sing to the LORD,
>   because he has dealt bountifully with me.

Why the change of heart? Why the dramatic shift in tone? Have we missed a piece of the story? Did the scribe's pages get stuck together as he was copying from one papyrus to the other? Maybe so. Or maybe something happened off-stage that brought the psalmist's waiting to a neat and tidy happy ending. Maybe the speaker has made it out of the waiting room.

But I'm not sure that's right. One little footnote in my study bible says that the word "trusted" is better translated "trust." That one change makes a world of difference: "But I *trust* in your steadfast love." *My enemies wait to celebrate my downfall, I wait for you to take notice of me and my suffering,* **but I trust**. What if the psalmist does not move from questioning God to trusting God? What if it's not either/or? What if this is all in the mix at the same time? What if the speaker is still in the waiting room? Then the psalm seems to be about more than a waiting room. Instead it seems to say that there is room in the waiting, room for doubt, sadness, trust, anger, and hope. The waiting room, the waiting place or space can hold it all, can hold *us* all no matter what brings us here. The speaker points to a memory of God's faithful, steadfast love. This love held him once and holds him still, even as he waits and wonders and wrestles aloud, even as he learns to wait, even as he shows us how to wait.

It is not easy to wait alone. In the experiment I mentioned, the woman seems visibly uncomfortable when she is left to respond to the random tone all on her own. Once another waiting one arrives, she carries on what she has learned, and soon her new waiting room colleague is standing on cue as well. The life of faith is not a silly Candid Camera experiment. There are no arbitrary rules about sitting and standing, no one faithful way to wait. And so we wait. Some of us are waiting for answers. Some of us are waiting for an end to pain, for the healing of a relationship, for a new beginning, for light, for justice, for love, for hope, for peace. Some of us trust easily. Still others are wondering if trust even makes sense anymore. But we wait. And we wait together, held by this One who makes room for all of our waiting and for all of us.

Thanks be to God. Amen.

Light in the Darkness
Isaiah 9: 1-7

November 17, 2013

Deep darkness…thick darkness. One of the most haunting and powerful images from this first part of Isaiah is darkness. Darkness shows up in different ways, different times, and different places. Darkness creeps in after a death or a loss. Darkness rushes in in times of depression or despair. Darkness comes occasionally on the heels of a storm. When I was a junior in college, Hurricane Hugo skipped from the South Carolina coast up to the piedmont of North Carolina. Inland areas which only knew about storm surge and tropical winds from watching the evening news now felt the brunt of Hugo's nearly 100-mile-an-hour winds. The college was not as prepared as it should have been. Sturdy brick structures were able to withstand the bands of wind and rain, but massive trees were toppled and when everything stopped, we realized that everything was dark. The dorms had no emergency lighting. The Duke Power grid we relied on for electricity was down. It was dark. Administrators sent most students home, away from campus so that they wouldn't hurt themselves or one another. Darkness was one of their biggest concerns. We trip in the dark. We get lost in the dark. We can't see to help ourselves or anyone else in the dark. In a recent interview, a doctor in the Philippines commented, "It gets really dark at night."[46] It is difficult for me to imagine just how dark it must be in the Philippines now, how dark it must have been in the first days after Haiyan hit, especially at night. Sometimes it seems everywhere we look we hit darkness, everywhere we turn we hear bad news, everywhere we walk we are hemmed in by despair on all sides.

---

[46] http://www.nytimes.com/2013/11/14/world/asia/at-a-philippine-hospital-survivors-face-quiet-despair.html

Isaiah understands what it is to be surrounded by darkness and dead ends. A contemporary of Amos, Isaiah is speaking to a people who have been defeated. The people have struggled for years with corrupt kings, occupation by foreign nations, and confusion about whom to worship, whom to follow, and whom to serve. The northern kingdom has disappeared; the southern kingdom is under assault.[47] The darkness is strong and unyielding.

And yet…Isaiah offers some of the most hopeful and promising and familiar words in all of scripture. In the deep darkness, light has shined. The text tells us that it's already happened, that it's a done deal. And the light that has come is the result of the birth of a child, a new king. And the light has come into the very darkest corners of Israel—Zebulon and Naphtali, the front lines of occupation: "This new dawn arose in the very regions of northern Israel first annexed by [the Assyrians]."[48] In other words, the light shined in the very places that have been dark, hopeless, and defeated the longest.

Isaiah tells us that the light breaks forth with the birth of a son, a new king in the line of David, a king who is poised to be a new kind of ruler, a different kind of sovereign, a king with many titles. Many of us may begin to hum strains of Handel's *Messiah* when we hear those names. More of us associate this text with Christmas and the birth of Jesus, as well we should. As the early church looked back over God's history with the people of Israel, they could see how God's decisive work in Jesus fit into the larger, longer story. As we mentioned last week, prophets do not predict the future. They speak the word of God into their current context. They speak God's judgment on the people's sin, they confront the powers-that-be on their ruthlessness and corruption, and they offer God's hope to people in despair, people

---

[47] From the Sermon Brainwave podcast found here:
http://www.workingpreacher.org/narrative_podcast.aspx?podcast_id=444
[48] http://www.politicaltheology.com/blog/the-politics-of-the-child-isaiah-91-7/

mired in deep darkness. Here in Isaiah and elsewhere, prophets shed light on how and where God is at work in their midst bringing light in the midst of darkness and hope in the midst of despair. In the birth of a human king, Isaiah insists that God is at work bringing light, shining light in a weary world not in the far-off future, but at that very moment.

One of the gifts of walking through the Hebrew scriptures this fall has been the chance to remember and recognize that since the dawn of creation, God has been at work to seek out the people of God and to restore us to right relationship with God and one another. It happens through Abraham and Sarah; it happens through Moses; it happens and keeps happening, because God is faithful and persistent and stubborn and tireless. God is zealous, even. God works and keeps working through human beings to do this reconciling and redeeming work. As one scholar insists, "God is always recruiting human agents to enact the Great Reversal about which God [has] persistent zeal."[49] Any light that shines, any action that pushes back at the darkness, is fueled and inspired by a God who is fiercely determined to defeat the darkness, to bring an end to despair. And, by the grace of God, the lights still find a way to shine.

Thanks to a friend, I was introduced to a project known as "The Light of Human Kindness." Begun by a woman in Richmond, Virginia, the project collected individual stories of darkness and light:

> [Stories] about needing hope or light during a dark time and what kept [people] going. [People were invited to] share a memory of someone important to [them] who gave [them] something to hold on to at just the right moment.[50]

The stories recount moments of deep darkness ranging from abandonment, homelessness, PTSD, addiction, and depression. The

---

[49] Walter Bruggemann, *Isaiah 1-39*, Westminster Bible Companion, p. 85.
[50] http://thelightofhumankindness.tumblr.com/

stories also highlight moments when light punctured the darkness through the action of other human beings, friends and strangers alike. The stories were then written on an 80-foot wall of a building in the middle of town and transformed into a mural. 1000 lights were then installed. There are two ways to light up the installation. Both happen through the wonders of modern technology:

> [People] from around the world are currently performing acts of kindness and recording their experiences on [the web site]. Each act completed and recorded powers up an individual light in real time…When you hit 'submit,' you light the wall![51]

The other light moment happens in person:

> The mural…invites folks to experience the power of human connection by interacting with the wall itself using conductive properties and other cutting-edge technology. The collective energy of one hand touching the wall while linked with a physical human connection to others also powers the lights in an amazing display of our shared capacity to light the world.[52]

In the wake of hurricanes and typhoons, in the aftermath of tragic deaths and disasters, quite often, too often in fact, the darkness seems too deep, too thick, and yet by the grace of God and through the persistent work of God, light can and does pierce the darkness. And it happens through the work of human beings. Our kindness, "our [God-given] shared capacity to light the world" does not banish the darkness, but by the grace of God our light reflects God's light and in small but powerful ways manages to hold the darkness at bay.

One strength of this installation in Richmond is that it is placed quite intentionally right in the middle of a well-worn part of town, on the

---

[51] http://thelightofhumankindness.com/about/
[52] http://thelightofhumankindness.com/about/

side of a well-worn building. Isaiah reminds us that that is how God works as well. God does not reach down and lift us up and away from all that is messy and messed up in the world. God does not do an end run around our brokenness or sidestep our broken ways. Rather God works to transform the messy and messed up world through the work of messy and messed up human beings. In a shining moment, God takes boots and bandages and uses them to fuel a fire to warm our hearts and light our way. In a shining moment, God uses battleships to bring food, medicine, water, and personnel that offer help and hope to the Philippines.[53] The story is not over. Darkness still stands at the ready. We will mess up; we will sidestep God's way; we will get lost. But the God of Israel remains faithful; the God we meet in Jesus Christ remains zealously determined. Our God does not hide from the darkness. Our God is not thwarted by our messes or our messed-up ways. Our God will not rest until our God makes a way for peace, a way for hope, a way for justice, a way for light—for us and through us, for all and through all.

Thanks be to God. Amen.

---

[53] http://www.theguardian.com/world/2013/nov/10/hegel-marines-typhoon-aid-philippines

Palm Monday
Matthew 21:1-17

April 14, 2019

In our first reading this morning, we heard that Jerusalem was in turmoil. Something about Jesus has this effect on Jerusalem. This language echoes Jesus' first arrival when the magi come looking for the newborn king: "When King Herod heard this, he was frightened, and all Jerusalem with him."[54] And now as Jesus makes his way into Jerusalem on a borrowed donkey, the city is once again all riled up, or perhaps it has not stopped being riled up. In fact Jerusalem has been troubled and unsettled for years. A colleague points out:

> The Roman occupation of Israel was a brutal fact of everyday life…Farmers, barely able to raise enough to feed their families, paid 25% of their harvest to Rome every two years and 10% of their harvest to the Temple every year. Enormous amounts of resources were taken from the people of Israel to benefit the Roman Empire…

> The Israelites were particularly hard for the Romans to pacify. Central to the identity of Jewish people was (and is) the story of the Exodus where God delivered the people from a brutal empire ruled by Pharaoh…By the time of Jesus, people were increasingly expecting liberation from the Roman Empire just as they had been liberated from Egypt. The annual Passover celebration (the story of Exodus retold) often turned into a time of social unrest and calls for liberation, especially in Jerusalem.

---

[54] Matthew 2: 3, NRSV.

By the time of Jesus, violent riots were such a regular feature of the season of Passover each year that the Roman governor, Pontius Pilate had begun to make it a practice every spring around Passover to leave his headquarters in Caesarea fifty miles away to the west and travel those fifty miles across the countryside and process through the streets of Jerusalem to his palace there.[55]

So Jerusalem is an unsettled place, and here comes this prophet from Galilee, the Prince of Peace, or the Son of God riding on a donkey, depending on whose view you take. Kings were known to ride donkeys during times of peace. Horses were reserved only for war and for processions of might and power. It could be said that a king who fears no threat rides a donkey. Jesus knows what kind of king he is, and he knows what kind of kingdom he comes to usher in. He comes in peace to usher in peace. He does not, however, come to make nice. It's an important distinction, especially for one who comes not simply to herald a coming kingdom in some faraway heaven in the distant future. In Jesus, the kingdom of heaven has come near. He has urged his disciples to pray for and work for God's kingdom come *on earth*, not far removed but here where tyrants rule and the least of these are still hungry, imprisoned, and sick. And in Matthew's timeline, he comes on a Monday.

This realization messes with our neat and tidy timelines, of course. Palm Monday doesn't have quite the same ring to it. I think we'd be hard pressed to get enough people to wave palms and sing "All Glory, Laud, and Honor" tomorrow morning because it is a Monday after all, with all that comes with Mondays—jobs, bills, appointments, meetings, reviews, pink slips, and parking tickets. In Matthew's telling it is not just any Monday; it is the Monday ahead of the Passover celebration in Jerusalem. Estimates suggest that the population of

---

[55] Dr. Ron Byars quoting the Rev. Ron Luckey, an ELCA pastor

Jerusalem at the time was normally around 50,000 people. That number was believed to swell upwards of 125,000 to 150,000 during Passover. One might argue that this made for more of a manic or frantic Monday. More people require more resources. More people mean that the streets and the Temple would be more crowded. Tensions are already high. Pilate has likely arrived with his warhorses and soldiers in tow. If riots are commonplace, and if the story of Passover is in the air, one can only imagine what kind of Monday it must be. And then Jesus comes into the mix, the rabbi from Galilee who has just healed two blind men in Jericho. Their cries to him, calling him the Son of David, still linger in many of his followers' ears, pointing to him as promised Messiah, the long-awaited king who will reclaim the throne of his ancestor David and save them one and all. Jesus knows that the city is in turmoil, quaking and rumbling the Greek suggests, the same word that gives us the word seismic. Jesus is not simply coming to enjoy a few moments in the limelight or to pacify the hungry masses. Jesus is coming to confront all that has undermined and corrupted the life and worship of the people, to make right what is wrong, to make whole what is broken, and to break the hold the elite have on all that is good and all that is sacred, to take on the brutality that has become a fact of everyday life.

And so, yes, he carefully scripts the ride in on a humble donkey, once again making the explicit connection to a passage from Zechariah, emphasizing that he is the promised one, the one the prophets hoped for and longed for, the fulfilment, the in-the-flesh presence of the very God who has pursued and rescued the people for generations. And now, this Jesus has come to Jerusalem to confront and confound all that oppresses the people. And again, he does not come to make nice or to make people be nice.

And in Matthew's account, he heads straight for the Temple where he turns over tables, calls out those who have warped the worship offered there, and then turns to healing the blind and the lame. These are disruptive acts. But they are not simply stunts pulled for shock value alone. They are a judgment on a system that churns along for the benefit of the powerful and at the expense of the least of these. And Jesus will have none of it. And did you notice? The act that draws the ire of the chief priests and scribes is not the turning over of the tables but the acts of healing and the children's crying out, "Hosanna to the Son of David." It's one thing to borrow a donkey and topple a few tables; it is another thing entirely to upend the way they have always done it and to question the very heart of Temple life, to call out the systems that conspire to oppress and demean those who do not sit in power or wear the fancy robes. And now is not the time to make nice or play by the rules. Jesus knows that his time is as limited as the leaders' patience. He will not get out of this confrontation alive, so he uses his moment to give new life to others, the way God always intended for the community of faith to do.

And so I wonder, what would Jesus upend if he marched into the church today? What would he disrupt or rattle to call us on the carpet? What would he say about our Sunday ways and the part they play in the Monday world? As I stand here in my fancy robe with my pretty stole, I realize I am more likely to play the role of the priest than of the children crying out from the shadows. And Monday's coming, not just for me but for everyone, with its struggles and injustices getting in the way of Jesus' kingdom come and coming on earth. We give what we can to One Great Hour of Sharing. We bring toilet paper and socks and canned goods. We count out our coins and roll up our sleeves to help where we can, but I wonder if that is all the church can do. Yes, we feed the hungry and tend the sick, but I can't help but wonder if Jesus wants us not simply to patch up those harmed by the system but to question and transform the system itself.

My friend and colleague Pen Peery writes:

On a bench outside St. Alban's Episcopal Church in the quiet and quaint (and affluent) town of Davidson, NC a man lies draped in a blanket. His face is covered. He could be any one of the millions of the homeless poor who take sleep when they can get it, except for the fact that upon closer inspection this man's feet are pierced, evidence of the fact that he has been crucified.

The parish installed the provocative statue called *Jesus the Homeless* [in the spring of 2014]. It is the first of three of its kind to be [installed] in the United States. Soon after the statue made its debut a woman from the neighborhood called the police to report suspicious activity. Another neighbor filed a complaint and wrote a letter to the editor of the local paper because the statue 'creeped him out.'[56]

[Pen says,] Sometimes I worry that the Jesus I proclaim doesn't creep people out enough.

If there were really two parades that entered Jerusalem at Passover that year, sometimes I wonder if I am spending my energy on making sure the one with horses has everything they need to be comfortable instead of laying my cloak out for the man coming down the hill from the Mount of Olives.[57]

I often share Pen's worry. So often we encourage those crying out for justice and healing to wait their turn, to follow protocol, to work through the system. But Jesus has no patience for the system, not when it only benefits the ones who have shaped it in the first place, the ones who hold all the cards and call all the shots. Jesus is the Prince of Peace, not the Prince of Nice. He disrupts and confronts and upends

---

[56] http://www.npr.org/2014/04/13/302019921/statue-of-a-homeless-jesus-startles-a-wealthy-community

[57] Pen Peery from his paper for the Well, 2014.

everything. He heals those who aren't even supposed to be in the Temple, the ones who quite possibly creep everyone out, the broken, the battered, the lost and the left out. He has no time for my decent and orderly ways, not at the expense of those who are crying out for justice and mercy. And as uncomfortable as that may make me, it is good news. Because in the end, it is not my robe or my degrees or my making nice and following the rules that saves me. It is this Jesus, the one who breaks into my pretty Sunday ways to turn my Monday world upside down who saves me. This one who is betrayed and handed over on a Thursday, crucified on a Friday, is ultimately raised on Sunday to save us all. And the everyday world is never the same, or at least it shouldn't be.

In the name of the Father and of the Son and of the Holy Spirit. Amen.

Miracle Machine
John 2:1-11

January 14, 2018

A few years ago, I stumbled across a Kickstarter campaign for the Miracle Machine. Developed by experts in fields of wine and technology, this genius invention was designed to turn water into wine on your countertop, just by adding a few ingredients. You choose your wine preferences: fruity or dry, bold or smooth. Better yet, it would be finished in three days—downright biblical. And, you could even monitor the wine's development using an app on your phone. Simple. Elegant. Convenient. All for $499. Sign me up.[58]

The truth is that quick-fix countertop wine is not going to solve the problem. When the wine has completely given out, when we, when those we love are running on fumes, no quick fix is going to make a difference, not the difference we truly need. There are chasms that wine cannot fill, holes that wine cannot fix. But this text from John is about more than the wine.

The text is of course, Jesus' first miracle in John, the first public revelation of who he is—sort of. He has been baptized, and he has called his first disciples. Now he finds himself at a wedding. And his mother—who is never named in John—makes it clear that she expects him to address the whole out-of-wine problem. And after a bit of surly backtalk as my mother would have called it, he does. He tells the servants to fill these huge jars with water, and they fill them to the brim. And—as one scholar points out—it's not as simple as pulling out the garden hose and turning on the spigot. It's likely "a laborious task, depending on where the nearest water source is."[59] Miracles

---

[58] http://time.com/14229/miracle-machine-water-into-wine/
[59] http://leftbehindandlovingit.blogspot.com/2013/01/the-sign-of-hour.html

require a bit of work behind the scenes, or at least this one does. Miracles don't just happen, or at least this one doesn't. Until it does. The jars overflow—thanks to the servants—and suddenly there is an abundance of wine, the equivalent of 730 bottles.[60] Scholar Karoline Lewis points out that:

> The details of abundance cannot be overlooked in this text— six water jars, each 20-30 gallons, filled to the brim, of the best wine. The amount in and of itself is extraordinary. But the best wine? At this point in a wedding celebration? Unheard of. Back in the day, weddings typically lasted a week, where the host would serve the better wine when the guests could actually taste what they were drinking, a nice Sonoma-Cutrer Russian River Chardonnay, perhaps. Only after a few days of drinking and determined levels of inebriation would the guests be served the Franzia box Merlot or Gallo jug Chablis. [And then she asks,] Where have you experienced that kind of grace?[61]

Dearly beloved, we are gathered here today in mid-January. With the exception of Friday's crazy spring-like temperature spike, it's pretty gray everywhere, and it will be gray for a while yet. The parties are done, and everyone's pants and budgets are tighter than we'd like. False alarms and real news send us running for cover. And miracles are in short supply.

We could use a miracle machine about now. I'd really like to be able to make miracles. It doesn't have to be water into wine. I'll take a cure for the young woman trapped in the stubborn grip of mental illness. I'll take good news for the spouse who is facing down his own mortality even as his beloved spouse is lost to dementia. I'll take a home for the family who can barely scrape together enough money for rent and food

---

[60] http://www.seetheholyland.net/tag/stone-jars/
[61] Lewis

even as the parents work five jobs between them. I'd like an end of the opioid epidemic that is decimating families and communities nationwide. I'd like a machine that generates miracles like those.

In John the miracles are not called miracles. They are signs. And these signs "point to a truer revelation about Jesus."[62] They give us hints about who this Christ is and what he comes to do and be. They give us a fuller picture of this one who is full of truth and grace. Karoline Lewis notes that the gospel of John only mentions grace by name four times and only in the prologue. She wonders:

> What if we take the incarnation seriously and suggest that once the Word becomes flesh, the rest of the Gospel shows you what grace tastes like, looks like, smells like, sounds like, feels like?[63]

That's what these signs do after all. They begin to show us what grace tastes like, looks like, smells like, sounds like, feels like. I have no miracle machine; I am no miracle machine; I cannot manufacture miracles, but I can point out signs that give me a taste or a glimpse or a whiff of abundant grace.

I can point to Dade Middle School in Texas. The staff worried that they would be short about 50 mentors or dads for a Father-Son breakfast, so they put out an appeal on Facebook. They would have been thrilled to have 50 show up. Instead 600 men volunteered. They talked about careers. They taught the boys how to tie a tie. School officials have seen improvements in test scores and behavior. The bounty of that one day has overflowed into the lives of young people who are too often overlooked or written off.[64]

---

[62] Lewis

[63] Karoline Lewis, http://www.workingpreacher.org/preaching.aspx?commentary_id=1556

[64] https://www.facebook.com/NowThisNews/videos/1762872707136179/

I can point to a moment on a train in Chicago last week. Jessica Bell writes:

> So I'm headed home on the CTA Redline and there's a homeless man sitting across from me. He's older, weathered, minding his own business. His feet are so swollen he's wearing the tattered gym shoes he has with the back folded down; like slip-ons. I don't know how many pairs of socks he's wearing in an attempt to keep his feet warm but there is blood seeping through. There's another man on the other side of the doors; younger, carrying a satchel and a suitcase, also minding his own business. He's wearing a pair of big black snow boots. They look new; they look expensive; they're built for a Chicago winter.
>
> Quietly, in a blink and you'll miss it fashion, the younger man takes off the boots he's wearing and passes them to the old man. He opens his suitcase and gives him a pair of socks as well. The young man puts on a spare pair of shoes from the suitcase. These shoes are nice too, but not as nice as the boots. They would have fit the old man just as well, but they were not what this old man needed.
>
> He tells the old man to try and clean his feet and to make sure he changes into the new socks as soon as he can and then the young man gets off at 87th. Those of us who are close enough to see and hear the exchange are floored. The shoes off his feet.[65]

I can point to Dr. King. Tomorrow we remember the legacy of this young preacher from Atlanta who inspired men and women of all ages, backgrounds, and races to embrace a vision of a better nation. He was

---

[65] https://www.facebook.com/jessica.bell.13/posts/998113405762 as shared by Michael Kirby.

not perfect, and he was written off by many in his day as a rabble rouser and a communist. And yet Dr. King tirelessly called a nation to account for its ugly past and its unfulfilled promises. Sadly, we still have many miles to go, but there is a renewed passion for honest conversation about the challenges of being black or brown in our beloved nation and there is sleeves-rolled up work being done to face our past and our present in hopes of shaping a different future for our children. That looks like grace to me.

No, I can't make miracles, but I can point to them, and in some small way, like the servants who filled those jars, I may be able to be a part of one.

As it turns out, the Miracle Machine was not all it promised to be. In fact, it was a hoax. And the promoters admitted it. They were in cahoots all along. The press release announcing the hoax read:

> Internet sensation the 'Miracle Machine,' the first affordable wine making device for the home, is not a real device – it is just a piece of wood. The fictitious miracle, fronted by wine entrepreneurs Kevin Boyer and Philip James of CustomVine, has generated extensive media coverage around the world since its unveiling nearly two weeks ago. The disruptive program concept was initiated as a **pro-bono campaign to support not-for-profit 'Wine to Water,'** an organization that provides people around the world with access to clean water, one of life's basic necessities.[66]

Ultimately, they weren't interested in creating quick-fix wine but in making every day, run-of-the mill, life-restoring miracles. They mention that the launch was disruptive, but miracles often are. Only a few at that wedding know what Jesus does, but for the ones who are

---

[66] http://www.businessinsider.com/lot18-founders-miracle-machine-is-a-hoax-2014-3

in the know—the ones who tasted that wine, the ones who saw him behind the scenes, the ones who filled those jars—their lives are never the same. Soon he'll be turning the tables, healing the sick, and disrupting the entire world. It will taste like the very best wine. It will sound like the laughter of one who has been healed. It will smell like fish cooked over a campfire and freshly baked bread. It will look like the kingdom of God. And it will feel like home.

And along the way when it looks like the wine might give out again, when Christmas seems too good to be true, when Easter seems like a hazy dream, Jesus will still find a way to show up and work a miracle in some old clay jars, in a cool drink of water in a remote village, in a hard conversation with a neighbor whose face looks different from mine, in the face of a stranger-turned-mentor, or even in a pair of second-hand boots.

Thanks be to God. Amen.

Friends and Neighbors
John 13:1-17

February 25, 2018

The religious leaders have been suspicious of Jesus all along, but it is the raising of Lazarus in last week's text that serves as the final straw. They have realized the threat he poses to the status quo, and they are determined to bring him down. In chapter twelve Jesus shares a meal at the home of his friends in Bethany and Mary anoints his feet. The leaders get wind of this visit and plot to kill Lazarus, since his being raised has been the reason for many more people to follow Jesus. Jesus then rides into Jerusalem on the back of a young donkey while the crowds wave palm branches on Palm Sunday.

Our text this morning brings us to the heart of Holy Week, the days between Jesus' triumphant entry and the first Easter morning. To this point, John has moved at a fairly steady pace. He will now slow down, asking the listener to move more slowly through Jesus' final days. In this morning's text, we meet Jesus at table with his disciples sharing a final meal. [Read John 13:1-17]

I have never lived in a world without *Mr. Rogers' Neighborhood.* This past week, as you may have heard, the iconic children's show celebrated its 50th birthday just a few months before I reach mine. My father used to talk about coming home at the end of a stressful day to find my brother and me seated in front of Mr. Rogers with our thumbs in our mouths. Dad said it made him want to do the same, to be comforted and encouraged and told that he was special. We Presbyterians love to brag that Fred Rogers was one of us, that he was a Presbyterian minister. He went to seminary part-time while he worked at the fledgling public television station in Pittsburgh. Once he graduated, he was ordained and could have served in a traditional parish setting, but he had found his ministry, his calling in children's television. He felt strongly about taking children seriously and speaking to them not only about how to tie their shoes but to encourage them to talk about difficult topics such as divorce and death. Through his gentle voice and faithful ways, he shaped generations to choose love over fear, a radical notion that was born during one of the most polarized moments in American history. Mr. Rogers—armed only with a TV camera, a pair of sneakers, a cardigan, and his faithful imagination—helped children find a way not to hide from the storms but to move through them.

When we meet Jesus in our text this morning, a storm of another sort is brewing, and Jesus knows it. He also knows his time is short, so he gathers for a meal with his friends. John does not tell us what's on the menu or what the conversation is about. He simply tells us that Jesus knows that his hour has arrived and that he loves those at the table with him completely, fully, and without end. Without warning Jesus gets up, removes his outer robe, picks up a towel, and fills a basin with water. He begins to wash the disciples' feet.

As you may know, foot washing is a regular practice in the ancient world. Traveling around on foot wearing sandals made for tired, dirty, smelly feet. It was customary for a host to provide a bowl of water and a towel for the guest to wash his own feet upon arrival. In wealthy households, occasionally a slave would wash a guest's feet. It was intimate work. It was demeaning work. It was dirty work, and Peter resists Jesus' washing his feet with every fiber of his being. We so easily shake our heads at impetuous Peter: "Silly Peter. He of all people should know what Jesus is up to." But what if Peter refuses not because he doesn't get it, but because he does? His refusal is stronger than most translations convey. As my colleague Jarrett McLaughlin points out: "More literally Peter says, 'Never not can you wash my feet to the end of the age.'"[67] Peter's refusal is deeper than his not wanting his beloved rabbi to demean himself in this act of servitude. Peter seems to

---

[67] Jarrett McLaughlin in his paper for the Well, 2017.

understand that this act indicates a far more subversive movement that turns the world—and everything that Peter has known and understood about that world—upside down. This foot washing is not simply a gentle loving act, but a prophetic action that turns any purely sentimental or sweet notion of love on its head. In this act, Jesus eliminates any notion of hierarchy or privilege as marks of the kingdom of God. He will soon lay down not simply his power but his very life for his friends. He expects his friends to follow his example and do the same. Jesus is not simply calling his disciples to be gentle and loving inside the safety of that room. He is calling them to serve each other in the same way, to show a world that keeps score and insists on hierarchies and winners and losers that in Jesus Christ there is a better, different way.

One of the most striking episodes of Mr. Rogers' show was one that featured a scene with his friend and neighbor Officer Clemmons. Rogers had heard Clemmons sing in church and asked him to play a police officer on the show. Clemmons resisted at first. As a black man raised in a violently segregated world, Clemmons says that he did not have the most positive view of police officers, and he did not want to play one on TV. But Mr. Rogers persisted. (I imagine it would be hard to tell Mr. Rogers "no.") Clemmons played that role for 25 years. There is one episode in particular that stands out. It takes place on a hot day. Mr. Rogers—still wearing his signature cardigan—is cooling off resting his feet in a pool, a plastic baby pool like the one my parents bought for my brother and me at the local Ben Franklin Five & Dime. He invites Officer Clemmons to join him. The show aired on the fifth anniversary of a Wade-In in St. Augustine, Florida when a group of young people—black and white—waded into a whites-only hotel pool. The owner of the hotel responded by pouring acid into the pool. The young people were dragged out and arrested while the world watched. So Clemmons knew full well that by showing his brown feet and Mr. Rogers' white feet in a pool together was a significant visual. But then it was time for Officer Clemmons to move on, and Mr. Rogers picked up a towel and helped him dry his feet. Clemmons said he was not prepared for the way that scene moved him. As he dried Clemmons's feet, Fred Rogers can be heard saying, "Sometimes just a minute like this, will really make a difference."[68] Rogers' meaning was clear. Yes, a dip in some cold water can be helpful on a hot day, but more importantly, a white man and a black man sitting together as friends and a white man drying and caring for his neighbor's brown feet is a prophetic moment that shows the world a different way. Such a moment can begin to unravel racism's tight clench on a world in turmoil because it shows children a different way.

I know it's only Mr. Rogers. It's only a quaint little children's program with a corny guy in a cornier cardigan. It was well before cable and YouTube, long before such things went viral, and yet, Fred Rogers was more than a kindly idealist. He knew the power of media; he knew the power he had to shape even a small corner of the world by following the example of the one who calls us his friends. He intentionally spoke with kindness to everyone, children included. He was careful not to discount anyone. He never called names. He welcomed everyone. All in an effort to follow Jesus and shape the world he knew in a faithful way.

To celebrate the anniversary, PBS is showing old episodes of his show. There will be a Mr. Rogers stamp, a documentary, and apparently Tom Hanks is set to play Rogers on the big screen soon. I'm guessing Fred Rogers would not want all the fuss, but I think we could use all of the Mr. Rogers we can get right about now. In his farewell to his TV audience in August of 2001, Mr. Rogers said:

> I know how tough it is some days to look with hope and confidence on the months and years ahead. But I would like to

---

[68] https://storycorps.org/podcast/storycorps-462-in-the-neighborhood/

tell you what I often told you when you were much younger: I like you just the way you are. And what's more – I am so grateful to you for helping the children in your life to know that you'll do everything you can to keep them safe. And to help them express their feelings in ways that will bring healing in many different neighborhoods. It's such a good feeling to know we're life-long friends.[69]

Jesus will soon say goodbye to his friends. They will not immediately follow the example he set. They will betray him, abandon him, and deny him, and yet, he still counts them as his friends; he loves them fully, to the end. We too find ways to betray him, abandon him, and deny him. Sadly, we still struggle to follow his example, too. We write off grieving students and frightened parents. We discount struggling leaders and demonize enemies. We allow our anger, our fear, and our opinions to guide us more than this One who washes our feet and lays down his very life to save ours. And still, he claims us as his friends. He shows us that there is a better way. And he knows that the world is watching to see how we—the ones who bear Christ's name—treat our friends and heal our neighborhoods.

Francois Clemmons recalls a day when he watched Fred Rogers film the final scene of an episode:

And you know how at the end of the program he takes his sneakers off, hangs up his sweater and he says, 'You make every day a special day just by being you, and I like you just the way you are?' I was looking at him when he was saying that, and he walks over to where I was standing. And I said, 'Fred were you talking to me?' And he said, 'Yes, I have been talking to you for years. But you heard me today.'[70]

---

[69] http://lybio.net/mr-rogers-goodbye/people/
[70] https://storycorps.org/podcast/storycorps-462-in-the-neighborhood/

Jesus has been calling us his friends for centuries. He has been calling the church to follow his example for millennia. He has been talking to us for years. He has promised to love us to the end. By the grace of God, may we hear him today. In the name of the Father and of the Son and of the Holy Spirit. Amen.

Open Doors and Purple Crayons
Acts 14: 27-15: 18

May 14, 2017

Last week, we met Philip in the middle of nowhere as he ran alongside the Ethiopian. The two talked about scripture and the story of Jesus. Then the Ethiopian was baptized and welcomed officially into the family of faith. On the heels of this encounter, we meet up again with Saul—who comes to be known as Paul. Chapter nine details Paul's dramatic encounter with Christ on the Damascus road. The very one who had "[breathed] threats and murder against the disciples" has now been transformed into one of the new Christian community's greatest champions. This morning's text brings us alongside Paul and Barnabas as they return to their home church in Antioch fresh from their successful mission in Pisidia and Pamphylia.

[Read Acts 14:27-15:18]

Thank goodness for those first few verses. Without them, the discussion in chapter 15 can begin to sound like a very technical and picky debate. The description of Paul and Barnabas's inspiring travels shines light and gives life and meaning to the debate that unfolds. We meet Paul and Barnabas in the midst of a happy homecoming, a victory tour of sorts, celebrating the "door of faith God had opened for the Gentiles."[71] The good news is spreading, and God is clearly at work making a way. So Paul and Barnabas are hanging out with the disciples, and all is well and good—until the rules police show up.

It seems there's a concern about everything's being done decently and in order. The church is doing its best to keep up with the Holy Spirit since it blew in on Pentecost, but there are procedures to be followed.

---

[71] Acts 14: 27, NRSV

A committee has been sent from the home office to make sure Paul and Barnabas don't get too excited about these new converts before they read the fine print. Circumcision, they argue, is not an optional covenant add-on; it's required. Their *Book of Order*, their rule book, reads "shall" apparently, not "should" or even "ordinarily." It's easy for me to make light of these uptight rule enforcers, but I'm actually sympathetic. In fact in a very real way. I'm one of them. They are my people.

I have purchased one set of grown-up coloring pages, but they stress me out. I really want to stay inside the lines, and I'm not that strong of an artist. Staying in the lines has always been a big part of who I am. I'm the big sister who shoved my goofy brother down when he tried to do a puppet show with his face showing. Michael Keaton made me nuts when he drove the wrong way in the carpool line in *Mr. Mom*. I was chiming in with the moms and the crossing guard who told him he was doing it wrong. It's one of the reasons I'm solidly Presbyterian. I've loosened up a bit in my middle years, but I don't hate rules or boundaries. In fact I still kind of like them.

There are many options in the ancient world. Lots of gods to follow. Loads of places to go on a Sunday morning, or not. Israel has always been the underdog, a 16 seed at best. They have made their way by sticking with the Lord of all, the one true God who has been ever faithful to them. They have not gone along with what's trending. Instead they have kept the Sabbath and followed the law. They have stayed inside the lines. That said, they are not strictly stuffy legalists, not simply members of the "we've-always-done-it-this-way" club. As another preacher says:

> Torah [or the law was never] a means of winning salvation. Jews knew that God is gracious and forgiving. For Luke, the law is not a means of salvation but rather [a way of showing one's] identity as a member of God's people…As other signs

of Jewish distinctiveness were destroyed, like their king, their land, and their Temple, Torah held people together. Torah was the Jews' joyful witness to the one true God in a world full of idols.[72]

Worshipping the one true God is not simply about following dry and dusty rules; it's also about knowing and claiming who they are as the children of that God, the people of Israel. The visiting committee doesn't have a problem with the Gentiles' coming to faith or becoming part of the family. Their concern is that they become part of the family "on the family's terms—through belief in the Word and gift of the Spirit."[73] Otherwise the family starts to change a bit; the very sense of who they are starts to shift. So the Jerusalem delegation is gatekeeping and trying to be faithful. They are happy to open the door, but they also take their jobs as doormen seriously.

"You make a better door than a window." I can't remember who said it to me first, but I have this vague memory of deep shag carpet and one of those big old console TV's, housed in a faux wood cabinet. I guess I had gone to change the channel and been so mesmerized by the show that I had stopped in front of the screen to watch, blocking everyone else's view. I didn't actually understand the saying at first so my getting out of the way was slowed by the fact that I had to figure out what the teasing comment meant before I actually moved. I can still feel the heat climbing up my neck when I finally figured it out. I got over that embarrassment, but the comment has stayed with me. There's a real difference between doors and windows, of course. Windows allow light to stream in or out; they allow us to see out or in, but they hold us at a distance—window shopping is not really shopping. Doors on the other hand serve as a boundary. They also

---

[72] William Willimon, *Acts, Interpretation* Commentary, (Atlanta: John Knox, 1988), 131.

[73] Willimon, 131.

serve as a way in. Luke tells us that God has opened a door to faith for these outsiders through Paul and Barnabas. The dilemma for the community is whether or not they will leave that door open or close it up and change the locks.

As I mentioned I prefer to stay inside the lines. I like the precision of a good ballpoint pen, and I still use a pencil to underline in most books including my bible, just in case I mess up and need to erase or redo. As a child who followed the rules and always tried to color inside the lines, crayons posed more of a challenge. Unless they are brand new and pointy, they are not terribly precise, and forget about erasing. Now that I've confessed all this, it probably comes as no surprise that I never knew what to make of Harold and his purple crayon.[74] Harold does not stay inside the lines, nor does he erase. He draws his own lines and keeps on drawing and then follows those lines out into the world beyond his window to go on a grand adventure where he climbs a mountain, shares a picnic with a moose and a porcupine, and sails in his very own sailboat. Toward the end of his adventure, Harold is getting sleepy and wants to find his way home, so he looks for his bedroom window. As I read the story again, I found myself thinking, "Harold's looking for a window, but what he needs is a door." He doesn't draw one, but he finds one, sort of, because he doesn't get stuck on the outside looking in. Somehow, some way Harold's trusty purple crayon leads him back home and back to his room that has been there all along. The big purple line that led him out into the magical world of picnics and porcupines now leads him back home where he discovers the window that's been there all along. He then draws himself inside his bedroom, gets tucked into his bed, and gazes out at the moon. The window had always been there. He was just on the wrong side of it. He was looking for a window, but what he really

---

[74] Crockett Johnson, *Harold and the Purple Crayon*

needed was a door. And somehow with the help of his trusty crayon he found a way in.

My brother—the once-rogue puppeteer—is now a thoughtful, rule-following attorney. He too stays inside the lines; in fact he's probably a much more faithful rule-follower than I am. He is currently finished serving his first term as an elder on the session at our home church. Last fall, the session was scheduled to go on a weekend retreat to discuss a controversial issue facing the church. Their head of staff had preached multiple weeks of sermons on the topic, but my brother had missed most of them either ushering or working. He called me in a bit of a panic late on that Friday afternoon: "I'm not opposed, but how do you get around scripture?" He could see through the window where he wanted to be. He just couldn't find a way to get there. He had a window, but he needed a door. Thanks to the Holy Spirit and lots of other conversations, I heard myself blurt out, "You don't get around it. You go through it." It wasn't simply the answer *he* needed to hear; I needed to hear it again, too. I knew it of course but hearing myself say it out loud helped me find the door again. I didn't have to make up an answer or dodge the rules or draw a line skirting around scripture to be faithful. The door was there, and it was standing wide open. It took my faithfully rule-following brother to remind me. Together we walked through the very scripture he had feared that we needed to skirt, and it those words, *the* Word, together we found the open door that had been there all along—several doors in fact.

Paul and Barnabas have their debate and discussion with the Jerusalem committee in Antioch, then they make their way to Jerusalem to meet with the larger body. Along the way they encounter more open doors, more faith, more joy. They are met with open arms and yes, open doors when they get to Jerusalem, but some members of the council still want to insist on one door to faith for the Gentiles, a door that sticks with one tradition and one way in. But doors seem to be blowing open everywhere, whether the worried ones like it or not. Peter, a new convert to the door-wide-open party himself, flips the script. The open doors are not simply good news for the Gentiles. They are the best news for everyone. "We're not going to be left out," Peter assures them. "We believe that we will be saved through the grace of the Lord Jesus, just as they will."[75] In case we forget, grace is good news for everyone, Jew and Gentile alike. James, the revered leader of the Jerusalem church, the brother of Jesus himself, then leads the group through one more door that has been open all along. He follows a divinely drawn big purple line back to the prophet Amos and points to the God who has been drawing and creating wide open doors from the beginning:

> 'I will rebuild the dwelling of David, which has fallen;
>> from its ruins I will rebuild it,
>>> and I will set it up,
> so that *all other peoples* may seek the Lord—
>> even all the Gentiles over whom my name has been called.'
>> Thus says the Lord, who has been making these things known from long ago.[76]

The covenants have not saved them. The law has not saved them. The rules have not saved them. Their faithfulness has not saved them. The God who **keeps** covenant has saved them. The God who remains faithful has saved them. This God kicked open doors of shame to seek out the man and the woman as they hid in the garden. This God carved a door through the sea to free the Israelites from Egypt. This God rolled away that death-protecting stone to open the door to life on the first Easter morning. This door opening activity may still be new for us, but it is not new for God. God does not ask the Gentiles or the Jews or anyone else to be stuck on one side pressing our noses against

---

75 Acts 15: 11, NRSV
76 Acts 15: 16-18, NRSV, emphasis added

the glass. By the grace of God, the door to faith has been there all along, and by that same grace of that same God, that door is open even now, for rule-followers and renegades and everyone in between.

Thanks be to God. Amen.

Outside the Gate

Acts 16:1-15

June 30, 2019

"It almost didn't happen."[77] If Paul had continued on his journey as planned, he and Lydia would likely have never crossed paths. Paul has parted ways with Barnabas and is now joined by Silas and Timothy as he heads out again. It's funny though. He keeps trying to go places where God apparently does not want him to go. They repeatedly set their GPS for Asia, and yet, something—or more pointedly—some*one* stops them. The text does not tell us that they were frustrated, but it would make sense if they were. We don't know the details of the detours or what form they take; we are not told that there is a big neon sign or a more subtle nudge to change course. We are simply invited to come along as Paul and his traveling companions try to figure out where exactly God wants them to go next.

I've been fortunate enough to have done a fair amount of traveling, at least around Europe. I have done the touristy things, but some of my most memorable moments were detours of sorts. There was the lunch in a place filled with local Florentines where a man invited Dave and me to sit with him and then proceeded to order everything for us. He did not speak more than a few words of English, and we do not speak any Italian. I have no idea what some of the food even was, but it is still one of the best meals I have ever eaten. There was the dinner somewhere southeast of Paris where I gathered with other students one summer evening around couscous filled with fresh veggies from the farm where we were staying for the night. And there was the protestant church in that same village where this Presbyterian from Nashville, Tennessee found deep comfort in the familiar words in a

---

[77] As pointed out by Ronald Cole-Turner, "Theological Perspective," Acts 16:9-15, *Feasting on the Word*, Year C, Vol. 2 (Louisville: Westminster John Knox) 474.

new language inscribed on the spare church walls. Those words from the gospel of John offered a witness and a welcome I did not know I needed, a reassurance that God was there, too, without my having to pack God up in my backpack along with my passport.

Paul is always on the road, always in a new place meeting new people for the sake of the gospel. After a dream where a man pleads with him to come help him in Macedonia, Paul and the others head on their way and wind up in Philippi, a major city in the region. We are also told that it is a Roman colony, just in case we have forgotten how vast the reach of the Empire is. When they arrive, they make their way not to City Hall or the town square, but to a place of prayer, outside the gate. And there they find themselves in conversation not with a man but with a group of women, including Lydia. Lydia is a businesswoman, a dealer in purple cloth, a luxury item. Only the elite can wear purple, so Lydia's business weaves her in and among the 1%, but that does not necessarily make her one of them. The text also tells us that she, too, is an outsider, an immigrant to Philippi from Thyatira, hundreds of miles away. She is head of her own household, a rarity in the ancient world for a woman. And she is a God-fearer, a Gentile who believes in the God of Israel, but has not formally become part of the community. It's not clear that there is even a formal community for her to join; the Jewish population in cities this distant from Jerusalem remains small. A critical mass is necessary to have a formal synagogue, a quorum—or a minyan of ten adult males and yet, here is Lydia, along with these other women, outside the gate in the makeshift place of prayer, a synagogue of sorts. In a strange place, surrounded by unfamiliar faces and unfamiliar voices, Paul meets at least one person who shares his dearest devotion, his most fundamental identity: one who reveres and worships the one true God. They could not be more different: he is a zealous Jewish man turned wandering missionary for a crucified Savior; she is a female Gentile transplant who makes a living selling pricey goods to the Roman elite. And yet, in each other they find a common faith, a shared devotion. And this happens as they meet not in the Temple in Jerusalem, or in the midst of the movers and shakers, but on a riverbank, outside the city gate. All because his wandering and hers lead them there.

My friend and colleague Mary Ann McKibben Dana reminded me of a story about another wandering one, Columba:

> …a priest in sixth-century Ireland, who got in a rudderless boat and let God and providence take him where he was meant to be. He made landfall once but decided to push out again because he could still see his homeland on the horizon behind him. The second place he landed was Iona, the island where Christianity touched Scotland for the first time.[78]

I am a creature of habit. I tend to eat the same thing for breakfast every morning. I run the same routes and drive the same way to church most days. While I love traveling, in my everyday life, I do not tend to go where I cannot see something familiar. I do not wander much, and if I do, I rely fairly heavily on my trusty phone and some apps to tell me where I am. Seeing my home on the horizon behind me is like a safety net, a tether of sorts that helps me remember where I am and who I am. I cannot imagine getting into a rudderless boat and trusting the tides to take me where I need to go. And if I did, I sure as heck cannot imagine deciding that the first stop isn't quite far enough. I am quite comfortable within my circumscribed little world. I am not Paul; nor am I Lydia. Although I suspect I could learn something from both of them. Maybe the church could, too.

Because things look different beyond the horizon. And things look different outside the gate, wherever that gate may be, even if that gate, that dividing line, that wall is only a stone's throw away. I have grown

---

[78] Mary Ann McKibben Dana, in her paper for the Well 2013.

fairly familiar with the twists and turns in Allendale and College Park, but I haven't spent much time in the neighborhoods on the other side of Carlisle Road, unless I count Starbucks, McDonald's, or CVS, and no, those don't really count. I haven't spent any time in the laundromat or the nail salon. I confess that I do not know the names of anyone who works at Cedar Cliff Pizza or Subway. I could not tell you the names of any streets that wind around back there or even anyone who lives there, I don't think. Those places are not far away, but they are just enough outside my gate that they are almost as unfamiliar as that riverbank in Philippi. But I am certain that God is at work in the lives of people in those places. God doesn't need to go through me to get to them, but I wonder what I might learn if I ventured beyond the safety of my gate to go and see what God might be up to. Because it is not my home or my routines that define who I am or whose I am. It is Jesus Christ, the very one who always managed to be on the other side of the gate with others and outsiders. Shouldn't his church be there, too?

Like Jesus, Paul does not sit back and wait for people to come see him. He does not hang out or hole up and simply wait for Lydia to come his way. Instead he goes looking, curious and expectant to see where God is already at work. Because, Paul knows and trusts that God is already at work. He sees this work in Lydia, and in conversation with her, he is simply the one to share his story of his encounter with the risen Christ. It is a conversation, not a lecture. This conversation provides an opportunity for her to join the community, to confirm her faith in God by being baptized and being welcomed fully and formally into the family of faith.

One offshoot of my vocation is that when I tell people what I do, they quite often have a faith story or a church story to tell me, and quite often the faith story and the church story part ways somewhere. I wonder if that could be true in Lydia's case. I wonder who first told her about God, where she first learned of the Lord of all, and why it didn't go any farther than the riverbank. Maybe there was no formal Jewish community in Philippi or Thyatira. Or maybe it was something else. Did someone write her off because she's a woman? Was her independence a problem? Was her being an outsider or a merchant a threat? Or did she simply find her people, her community outside that gate and stay there?

This past week marked the 50th anniversary of the protests at Stonewall, when people of all different gender identities stood up to those who would sideline them, or worse. It also marked the 50th anniversary of protests in Harrisburg when the black community spoke up about racist policies and practices that led to despair, fear, and anger. Even 50 years later, bias, hatred, and alienation still face both communities. Lots of gates still remain. Everywhere. And we seem hell bent on constructing even more. I get it. We feel safer with gates. Inside them we find familiarity and comfort. Our gay siblings and our brothers and sisters of color still find themselves outside the gate in many ways, or at least on the other side from many of us. Yes, some gather there by choice, perhaps because they feel more at home there or because they feel seen or understood or simply safer there. Others gather there because they have received a lukewarm welcome or no welcome at all in too many churches. The same could be said of those who gather outside the gate due to poverty, mental illness, employment status, education, or age. And for all of our talk of welcome, I worry that our welcome falls flat—if it even makes it past those gates, if it ever reaches them at all.

In Lydia, Paul discovers not simply a new convert, but a companion in the faith, one who insists that he and the others make her home their home while they are there. In Lydia, Paul finds a place of rest from his wandering ways, an unexpected welcome, a home he did not know he needed. So maybe it is time for me—and even the church—to wander outside the gates a bit more, to trust that God is at work beyond our routines and regular routes, even down on the riverbank. Maybe it is time to step outside the gate, beyond the walls, and see what God is up to in the lives of those who do not look or love or live like me. Who knows? With these friends on the riverbank, with these companions outside our gate, we might just find faith unimagined. We might just discover a rest and a welcome we did not know we needed. We might just meet Jesus there.

In the name of the Father and of the Son and of the Holy Spirit. Amen.

Freed

Acts 16:16-40

July 7, 2019

She was really getting under his skin, working his last nerve we might say. She kept following them, kept shouting about who they were and what they were up to: "These people are servants of the Most High God! They are proclaiming a way of salvation to you!"[79] We've spent the past few weeks getting to know some of the less familiar faces in the book of Acts: Stephen, Barnabas, Lydia, and now we meet a slave girl and a jailer. We aren't told their names. Of course they have names, but for some reason the writer of Acts feels no need to tell us what they are. Instead we know them for what they do. She is a fortune-teller of sorts, who makes a lot of money for her owners. He is a jailer, in charge of the place where Paul and Silas are sent after they enrage the slave woman's owners by freeing her and rendering her worthless in their eyes. And at some point in the text, they are bound, prisoners in a way, as are Paul and Silas.

She quickly disappears off-stage. Once Paul calls the spirit out of her, we hear nothing more from her, just that her owners want payback for their loss of income. She only matters to them when she could make them a quick buck. Now that her gift has left her, she is no longer of any use to them. I wish we knew her name. I wish we knew what happened to her. So many scholars celebrate her being freed from her owners, her being liberated from this spirit that holds her captive. I want to celebrate, too, but I worry about her. I worry that though she has been freed from this one entrapment she is still just a throwaway, just another nobody who has nowhere to go, nowhere to be now that she is no longer generating a profit. I want to believe she is truly free

---

[79] Acts 16:17, CEB

now, but I cannot be sure she is because nothing in the text tells me it is so.

But then there is the jailer. His story is a bit more complete, a bit more fleshed out. We gather that he takes his job very seriously, that he wants to do it well. He wants to please his masters, the ones who hold his life and his livelihood in their hands. The Greek goes to great lengths to underscore just how thoroughly he locks up his prisoners. It is not simply a matter of locking the door; instead the text tells us, "He threw them into the innermost cell and secured their feet in stocks."[80] Everything is secure, locked up and pinned down, or as secure, locked up and pinned down as he can make them. Once the earthquake hits, we realize just how vulnerable the jailer is. Yes, he holds the keys to the prisoners' freedom, but he himself is not free. He is only of value to the empire as long as he does the empire's work, as long as he holds these others in check. When they are suddenly free, we see just how bound he actually is. And he does, too. He knows that his life is of little value to those who want the troublesome missionaries locked down and shut out from turning the world on its head. The empire can find another jailer. They can find another body to do the job. He is replaceable in their book. He is stuck. He is doomed. And he knows it. He sees no other way out, and he falls at Paul's and Silas's feet and begs, "What must I do to be rescued?"[81] His job won't save him. His bosses certainly won't either. He seems to think these free-in-a-different-way prisoners might be able to help him out.

They tell him, of course: "Believe in Jesus Christ, and you will be free." Other translations read, "Believe on Jesus Christ." Either way, they encourage him to put his trust not in the power plays of the lords of the empire but to build his life on the one true Lord of all, the Risen Christ, the One no empire can contain or defeat. And he does. And it

---

[80] Acts 16:24, CEB
[81] Acts 16:30, CEB

changes him. He is no longer simply the jailer but a freed and forgiven child of God who understands himself first and foremost as a freed and forgiven child of God. He goes from eking out a living to having a life. He still works the same job it seems, but it does not work on him the way it once did. And he goes from locking them in stocks to cleaning their wounds, from beating them with rods to welcoming them to his table.

Maya Moore has changed, too. Until this past winter, she had been all about basketball for as long as she could remember. Since she discovered basketball at the age of 3, she has been a shining star. She played for championship teams at UConn. She is now a superstar with the Minnesota Lynx and has been named the WNBA's Rookie of the Year and later the MVP. And yet, she walked away on a self-described sabbatical in February, because basketball, what she does, is no longer enough. It is no longer the entirety of who she is:

> She is answering what she says is a call from God. For most of her life, others have defined her: 'the Invincible Queen' and 'the Perfect Superstar.' Now she believes that God wants her to step away from the fray and consider what is truly important.[82]

In a way, she is stepping away due to burnout. The WNBA does not pay as much as the NBA, so Moore plays year-round in international leagues as well. But her sabbatical is not just a stepping away. It is a stepping toward, a stepping in. Moore is hoping to help free Jonathan Irons from prison. She is convinced that Irons—who is now 39—was wrongfully convicted at the age of 18 for a crime he supposedly committed at 16. The evidence was shaky. He was questioned without an attorney or a guardian. Irons makes no claims that he is a perfect

---

[82] Kurt Streeter, https://www.nytimes.com/2019/06/30/sports/maya-moore-wnba-quit.html

citizen; he had several misdemeanors on his record when he wound up in "the wrong neighborhood at the wrong time—in the wrong era" in January 1997 when a burglar broke in to a home and shot the homeowner in a predominantly white suburb of St. Louis.[83] Moore first became aware of his case when her godfather, a pillar in the community started examining Irons' case after getting to know him through a prison ministry at their church Moore and her family think of Irons as family. They refer to him as Big J.:

> She was shocked by the bare-bones facts. Irons was a poor African American teenager who had been tried as an adult and convicted by an all-white jury. The crime was violent and involved a gun, but no weapon was found. No blood evidence, no footprints and no fingerprints tied Irons to the crime. His 50-year sentence was handed down at a trial that ended when he was 18 — Moore's age [at the time].[84]

And now she is using her influence and her resources to see if she can help. And Irons is deeply grateful. He refers to Moore as "pure light" and as "a lifesaver who gives him hope."[85]

Moore seems lighter these days, even as she awaits news of whether a judge will reopen Irons' case. She sings in her church choir, spends time with her family, and serves in other ways in her community. She is no longer defined by her sport, by her job. Instead she is living into a larger calling, a deeper identity. Now free, she is working to help someone else be free as well. She has been saved. She has been rescued, and she sees Irons as a sibling and wants to tend to his wounds and help him find new life. And she is looking forward to welcoming him home, into her home where they can break bread and play another

---

[83] Streeter
[84] Streeter
[85] Streeter

round of checkers like they did when she visited him in prison as a teenager twelve years ago.

Like Lydia, the jailer responds to his baptism, his being claimed as Christ's own by opening his home and tending to his prisoners' wounds. He understands that his newfound freedom releases him from the fear of the empire and opens him to a life marked not by chains but by a table, not by fear but by generous hospitality, not by inflicting harm but by tending to wounds. Moore also understands that that is what her newfound freedom means. She is a child of the church, but her faith seems to have changed her in recent months. In 2016, following the deaths of Philando Castile and Alton Sterling, along with the shooting deaths of five police officers in Dallas, Moore could no longer remain silent. She says she found her voice and sensed a call to speak out for criminal justice reform. Moore's faith has been working in and on her, freeing her from fear of what others would say or what her future holds; her faith has freed her to work to free others.

We have spent the past week celebrating freedom, but our freedom in Christ goes far beyond anything listed in the Bill of Rights. Freedom in Christ is not something to be clutched or hoarded. Freedom in Christ is not contained by prison walls or restricted by national borders. Freedom in Christ is not in short supply, nor is it simply a frame of mind or a nice idea. Freedom in Christ does not permit us to sit silently by when any of God's children are in chains. Freedom in Christ abounds when it is shared and scattered.

Today we gather around the table. This table is not simply a place to gather with friends. It is a place to remember what our Savior suffered to free us from anything and everything that would bind us; it is a place to look forward to that heavenly banquet when we will gather with all of God's beloved ones from the farthest reaches and across the ages; and it is a place where we are nourished for the work of freedom now, the holy work of helping every single one of God's beloved children know what it is to be rescued, to be saved, to be free.

In the name of the Father and of the Son and of the Holy Spirit. Amen.

No Filter
Romans 5: 1-8

May 17, 2015

A few years ago, a friend convinced me to join Facebook, and I've had a love-hate relationship with it ever since. I love being in touch with my junior high soccer coach as well as friends from college and grade school. I get to see baby pictures and touching tributes. If the timing is right, I get updated on breaking news and discover important but less-hyped news stories. The challenge of course comes from the cranky posts and the self-righteous rants. I also grow weary of what's known as "vague-booking," when someone posts a dramatic status update with little detail. "Wow. I didn't see that coming." "Guess that part of my life is over." Of course there's the other extreme, the realization that we're not terribly honest on Facebook or other social media outlets. We post only the best pictures and only happy, shiny updates. My newsfeed is often filled with pictures of dream vacations, exciting job promotions, perfect smiling children in wrinkle-free, stain-free dresses, along with silly cat videos. I have now joined Instagram, which is all about the pictures and all about the filters. Using filters you can make your photo take on a vintage look, resembling the ones stacked in a drawer somewhere at my dad's house, photos of me with a bowl haircut and buck teeth with rounded corners and muted colors. Filters can make the pictures more dramatic, fuzzier, darker, lighter, or brighter, almost as if they were shot in vivid Technicolor. The filters make even me feel like an artist, and they sound downright exotic with names like lark, Juno, slumber, Perpetua, and willow. With just a tap of a finger, another layer is added, and the picture the rest of the world sees is changed for the better.

One would think that filters would make no sense to the apostle Paul. True, the thought of an iPhone would be foreign in the ancient world, but the human tendency to make things appear better than they are is nothing new. In Paul's world, struggles and suffering were understood to be signs of divine disapproval, or worse, punishment, so no one in her right mind would celebrate or boast about suffering. We hear Paul speak about this in other letters where he contrasts the wisdom of the world and the foolishness of the Christian faith: "For the message about the cross is foolishness to those who are perishing, but to us who are being saved it is the power of God."[86] Following a crucified Savior makes no sense in the empire, a realm where the weak are scorned and the strong are rewarded. So Paul's boasting makes no sense, to anyone's ears really, including mine if I'm honest.

I cringe at the "boast in our sufferings" language. If Paul isn't about filters or playing the make-everything-pretty game, why on earth is he boasting? Other translations that use *rejoice* or *celebrate* don't help me much here. Even if Paul's boasting gets us to some of the most beautiful words in all of scripture, I cannot find it in myself to boast in my sufferings, or those of anyone else, for that matter. As a chaplain intern in a hospital in Annapolis one summer in seminary, I was assigned to Labor and Delivery. I was thrilled at first, but I quickly realized that no one calls on a chaplain in L&D unless something is wrong. By the end of the summer I recognized that hospital chaplains are very special people, and that I was called to a wider span of ministry, one that includes unbridled moments of celebration to help temper the heartbreaking ones. If there was anything to boast about in those rooms on that floor, it was that I knew that the suffering and the struggles I met there were not the last word. That may just be Paul's point. It's not that we pull out the streamers and throw a party when suffering comes our way. Paul is not saying that we should. *Should* never makes its way in here, at least not in Paul's words. He does not say that we *should* boast in our suffering or that we *should* will our way to endurance or *should* get ourselves back to hope. He says instead that

---

[86] 1 Corinthians 1:18, NRSV

when we find ourselves in the midst of suffering, we can trust that endurance, character, and hope are on the horizon—not because of anything we do, but because of what God can do and promises to do in and through us. Because, let's face it, there are times we just cannot will ourselves along that path from suffering to endurance, to character to hope, and even if we do it's a pretty tricky path. When hope does come, it is only by the grace of God.

The media—social and otherwise—loves stories of gumption and happy endings, folks who persevered and triumphed in the face of tragedy. While I am all in favor of a good underdog story, I think Paul wants to make it clear that that's not what's at stake here. His eloquent words about hope, endurance and character come in the midst of a description of *God's* work of making things right again, *God's* work of justification:

> not of people who are strong, and character-filled, and hopeful, but justification of people who are weak, and broken, and in despair. That's who Jesus died for. Jesus died for people who strive for endurance, who try to be independent and strong, but who cannot be. Jesus died for people who try to have good character in the midst of bad circumstances, but who fall short again and again. Jesus died for people who try to concoct some easy hope for themselves, hope which does disappoint every time.[87]

God knows better than to fall for filters. God sees past the filters we try to put on our lives and works to make things right, not because we're good or faithful, but because God is good, and God is faithful.

---

[87] Mary Ann McKibben Dana, "Suffering, Endurance, Character, Hope," *Journal for Preachers*, January 1, 2005, 35-36.

Madison Holleran was a young woman who could not see past others' filters.[88] In high school, she was a star on the track and on the soccer field. After sorting through offers to play or run for different schools, she chose Penn. Her family knew she was struggling a bit that first fall. Her best friend from home knew it, too. In the end, there was nothing they could do. Madison died in January of 2014. Looking back, her friends and family still can't make sense of the disconnect they saw between a young woman wrestling with self-imposed pressure to be perfect and the young woman they saw on her Instagram account, an account brimming with inspirational quotes and happy, shiny pictures. Over winter break Madison got together with her high school friends for dinner. As they sat around the table, they talked about the challenges they had all faced in their first semester away:

> Emma…was running track at Boston College and having a hard time. Another friend…was playing basketball at Princeton and feeling overwhelmed. They had all shared some form of their struggles with Madison, yet in her mind, the lives her friends were projecting on social media trumped the reality they were privately sharing…

> [The writer goes on to say:] Checking Instagram is like opening a magazine to see a fashion advertisement. Except an ad is branded as what it is: a staged image on glossy paper. Instagram is passed off as real life.

> Yes, people filter their photos to make them prettier. People are also often encouraged to put filters on their sadness, to brighten their reality so as not to 'drag down' those around them. The myth still exists that happiness is a choice, which

---

[88] Kate Fagan, "Split Image,"
http://espn.go.com/espn/feature/story/_/id/12833146/instagram-account-university-pennsylvania-runner-showed-only-part-story

perpetuates the notion of depression as weakness. Life [itself] must be Instagrammed.[89]

Madison could not see past the filtered images on the screen, images that did not match the life she knew. This led her to think that the disconnect was her fault, that *she* was the failure, beyond hope, beyond saving. Some have asked where God was and is in all this. I also wonder where the church was and is. Unfortunately, too often, we Christians fall for the filters. We begin to believe or even profess that the life of faith should be as pretty as a picture on Instagram. Paul makes it clear that such delusions are wrong. As you may have heard, the American church has struggled with decline over the past few decades. In some cases we have played the filter game hoping that the right image would make us cooler, more relevant, more hip. We see huge shiny arenas filled with thousands of people clamoring to hear some sort of gospel promise of wealth and fame, and we want to jump on board. Many are buying it, but it's not the gospel Paul is selling. The unfiltered gospel message does not promise prosperity; the unfiltered gospel is more powerful than that, and the authentic, gospel-sharing church is already more relevant than any fad or fashion. I for one don't need a church that's cool, a church that has all the bells and whistles, a church that looks great on Instagram. Instead I need the church Paul envisions. I need:

> a church that might not look so cool on the outside, but is genuine and mission-oriented on the inside…a church that doesn't proclaim to get it right all the time, but is willing to *struggle together* to live as best we can together in Jesus' name.[90]

Paul does not play the filter game because he knows the power of the unfiltered Jesus, the one who dies not for those with picture-perfect

---

[89] Fagan
[90] Kathryn Zucker Johnston, pastor, Mechanicsburg Presbyterian Church, emphasis added

lives with Instagram-worthy images, but for those who are hurting, lost, broken, and embattled. In his suffering, in his death, we are reminded that nothing and no one stands beyond God's redemptive reach. In Jesus Christ, God seeks us out behind every filter we select and under every excuse we concoct to stand with us in our suffering, to help us endure, and to circle us back to hope. No filter needed.

Thanks be to God. Amen.

Under Grace
Romans 6:1-14

May 26, 2019

I've never met Anna McArthur, but I feel like we would be friends. She's a Presbyterian pastor and a mom, but more than anything she is honest about her life as she tries to do all the things. I recently came back across a blog post she wrote at the end of one of *those* weeks. In a blog post from October of 2016 she writes:

> I really thought my son was going to be admitted to the hospital for his pneumonia.
>
> We'd tried two different antibiotics. He was exhausted. Deep breaths hurt. Every time he'd tried to attend dance classes for the previous few weeks, he'd had awful coughing fits. He started wheezing sometime on Sunday. Antibiotics by I.V. seemed to be the next step. We had another follow-up appointment with the pediatrician Monday morning. So, I did what any reasonable mom would do on Sunday night: I baked six pies.
>
> Something is wrong with me.
>
> Thinking that my week was about to get turned upside down, I tackled something on my list. I was preaching on Sunday but was too flustered to write. I'd been given the 'money Sunday' of stewardship season and was feeling the pressure of the whole church budget. I was hosting the cross-country team on Friday night at our house for dinner. I knew I couldn't get my house ready yet. I knew I couldn't cook the pasta yet or get the salad going. So, I made dessert.

I forgot to add sugar.[91]

She goes on to say that the pies were awful and inedible, that she got crankier as the week went on, and that her eye started to twitch, a giveaway that all was not as well as she was pretending it was. She also writes that:

> [She was] treating God like an unwelcome guest, sighing and saying, 'Well, I guess you can ride in the car with me to go get the kids. We can catch up then if you insist.'[92]

The eye twitch was her cue to take a break and go to a yoga class, even though she did "NO TIME FOR IT." She headed to yoga because as she says:

> I have found grace before at yoga and hoped to find it there again. I was once in a class where the teacher started with, 'You will not be getting a grade in this class.' People laughed, but I knew she had my number. I felt relieved and then I felt sad because I'm actually pretty good at yoga and I wanted to get credit for doing something right. I'm a sucker for earning good grades. Most people know they aren't being graded in a yoga class. I sometimes forget.[93]

Me, too. But maybe it's heightened because the grading thing is in the air right now. As the end of the school year rolls around, I hear students and parents and teachers and grandparents worrying about end of grade testing, PSSA's, SAT's, and college acceptances. I also hear worried whispers from students who will be in summer school,

---

[91] https://annamcarthur.com/showing-upand-remembering-the-sugar/
[92] McArthur
[93] McArthur

the ones who need to repeat a grade, the ones who dread having to walk back in the door of that building or facing that one teacher.

And the grading does not end when we graduate. We are evaluated at our jobs. Judged on our parenting. Scrutinized for how we drive or how we look or how our children behave or what we weigh or the number of weeds growing in our yards. And those of us who consider ourselves to be people of faith are measured by the highest of standards. For years we have asked, "What would Jesus do?" and expect ourselves to do the same, and then we berate ourselves when we don't measure up. You may even know someone who no longer goes to church because he or she felt judged or flat out was judged because they did not measure up to the standard set before them by other church members or a pastor or even themselves. They may have found more grace in a civic club or a bowling team or a yoga class than they have in a place of worship. Maybe you've been there, too.

In today's text, Paul knows full well what it means not to measure up. As we read last week and as we say every week, all fall short. All means all. All miss the mark. And so some might argue that it's not worth even trying to measure up, that they might as well sin early and often, go big or go home in the whole missing the mark thing so that grace may abound. But Paul argues that to make that move is to forget what it means to be baptized, to forget what it is to be welcomed into the body of Christ. Baptism is a pivotal moment, Paul argues. Baptism is a moment we can point to, a moment when we recognize that the grace of God claims us, too. But many of us were infants when that water was sprinkled on our heads. Many of us were wriggling babies or babbling toddlers when our parents made those promises on our behalf. How on earth can we look back on that moment and remember a single thing? And if we can't remember it, how can it possibly be a reference point, a hinge or pivotal moment where we can see a before and after? Maybe if we could just go back and feel that water trickling down our necks or hear it sloshing in the font, maybe then we could hang on tight to the grace that baptism points us to. Maybe then we could fully grasp what our baptism means. Maybe.

The truth is that I'm not sure those who can remember their actual baptism ever fully grasp what that water means. Being aware of the water doesn't necessarily make us any better at remembering its power. And that's where Paul's words come in. He wants to make it clear that baptism makes a difference, not because the water is infused with special power but because the God who claims us in baptism is. In claiming us in baptism, God gives us a tangible reminder of what God is up to in Jesus. Paul makes it clear that in Christ we are made new, that the old life is gone, that a new life has begun. In Christ, Paul insists that God tramples everything else that wants to stake a claim on us, everything that wants to tell us we are not worth much without certain grades or degrees or accomplishments. In Christ, God overrides and overrules anything that dares to claim that our skin color or our grades or our bank account or our nationality or our gender or our age makes us less than. And yet those other voices are still strong. Those other voices are quite insistent and loud. By pointing us back to our baptism and our core identity as God's beloved children, Paul emboldens us to resist those voices and hear God's call to us and God's claim on us again.

And I need to be reminded, which is one of the reasons I love Stepping Stone Sunday.

I love that we give third graders new bibles so that as they continue to learn and grow, they have the chance to read for themselves and be reminded of the fierce love God has for all of humanity, for all of us and all of them. I love that we give our high school graduates blankets, tangible reminders of the love found here in this covenant community. As they wrap themselves in these blankets, it is our prayer that the blankets will remind them that of the grace God wraps around them not for what they have achieved but because of who they are and whose they are as God's beloved children, always and everywhere. And I love welcoming confirmands who wear stoles representing their gifts and their loves as they offer their whole selves to the Lord of all. Today they answer the same questions their parents or grandparents answered for them at their baptism. This moment draws them back to the font, back to the place where the church first told them that they are named as God's own forever. This moment blessedly draws us back there, too.

Each of these holy moments provides a touch point for them and for us. With the third graders we are invited to read God's word to and for us with new eyes. With the seniors we are invited to imagine God's love wrapped around us, too. With the confirmands we are called to hear the promises made at our baptism, to make those promises again ourselves. Each of these stepping stones gives us something to reach back to, to grab hold of. And each stepping stone calls us to remember that all of the falling short, all of the not quite measuring up does not have power over us now or ever because we are under grace.

Once in an interview, Bono, the lead singer for U2, was asked about his understanding of grace. He replied:

> Grace defies reason and logic. [It] interrupts, if you like, the consequences of your actions, which in my case is very good news indeed, because I've done a lot of stupid stuff.[94]

Haven't we all. A lot of stupid stuff and hurtful stuff and half-hearted stuff and hateful stuff. We've spoken when we should have listened. We've been silent when we should have said something. We have lashed out when our feelings have been hurt and fought back when our pride was wounded. We have measured ourselves by someone else's Instagram feed or new car or vacation photos or apparently

---

[94] https://noapologizing.wordpress.com/2011/02/24/u2s-bono-interview-about-christ/

blissful family reunion stories. We've been written off, turned away, given up, and had eyes rolled at us. We've also done our fair share writing off, turning away, giving up, and rolling our own eyes at others. And yet in Christ Jesus, we are "dead to sin and alive to God." We are under grace, not a free pass to do whatever we want, but an invitation to embrace the new life Jesus brings, an invitation to shape a life of courage, joy, kindness, and integrity, a life that extends grace to others. And when we fall short, grace is the gift that tells us we are worth infinitely more than our worst days and abundantly more treasured than our most shining moments. Under grace. Surrounded by grace. Grounded in grace. Washed and made new by grace. Now and forever.

Thanks be to God. Amen.

Convinced
Romans 8:26-39

June 2, 2019

I am convinced…How would you complete that sentence? I'd be quick to say that I am convinced:

> That chocolate is a health food, along with ice cream.
> That a baby's giggle is one of the holiest sounds around.
> That—given the chance—Steph Curry and I would be fast friends.
> That tears are exhausting and healing.
> That an ocean breeze is close to the breath of God.

My list tells you a bit about me, about what I like, what I feel, what I treasure, what I count on to be true. You can also probably tell that my list was written on a good day.

In a sermon preached at the National Cathedral in February, writer Michael Gerson spoke about his faith and about his struggles with depression. Two weeks before he was scheduled to preach, he was hospitalized for depression. In the depths of his disease, he had his own list of convictions that told him:

> You are a burden to your friends.
> You have no future.
> No one would miss you.[95]

While he later came to know his convictions were unfounded and wrong, the force of the disease was and remains strong. It is easy to be convinced that he is not worthy, that we are not worthy, that the world

---

[95] Michael Gerson, https://www.washingtonpost.com/religion/2019/02/18/i-was-hospitalized-depression-faith-helped-me-remember-how-live/

around us is headed in the wrong direction, and that what we do here and what we believe makes little to no difference.

In this chapter of his letter to the Romans, Paul shares a bit about his convictions, too. In this chapter we get a deep and thorough view of what it is that Paul truly believes. Paul understands that the Roman church faces extreme and extended hardship. He does not minimize the terrors they face as a community determined to worship Jesus as Lord and Savior. To profess Jesus as Lord is a political claim. If Jesus is Lord, Caesar is not. To make this choice, to serve Christ above everyone and everything else is to take a dangerous political stand. With this declaration comes persecution in ancient Rome and throughout the Roman Empire. So Paul recognizes the real danger in claiming Jesus Christ as Lord and Savior. He does not pat them on the head or promise sunshine and roses. After all, it is a danger Paul faces himself.

So he does not gloss anything over. No, he speaks of weakness, and of our inability in the midst of our struggles to find the words to pray. In the verses that come just before ours he speaks of hope, hope that cannot be seen or touched, because after all, hope that can be seen is not hope. By definition, Christian hope is hope that lies just beyond the horizon. And he boldly declares that:

> We know that all things work together for good for those who love God, who are called according to his purpose.[96]

We know. Yes, on our best days we do know this. On our best days we are convinced that God can pull redemption out of any situation—not that God is sending disaster and hardship our way, but that God is in the midst of us, in the midst of it all working for our redemption, working toward the new creation. But what about the other days? The

---

[96] Romans 8:28, NRSV

days when yet another mass shooting takes lives of people simply doing their jobs, days when children are separated from the parents because of their citizenship status, days when tornadoes rage and fires burn, days when the dementia makes her forget who you are, days when the addiction makes him steal from his own father, days when the pain runs so deep that you begin to wonder if God even cares at all. The pain we face is not the same as the struggles the Romans faced, and yet "hardship, distress... persecution...famine...nakedness... peril... [and weapons]" are still real threats for us and for all of God's beloved children.

Gerson says he has friends who see the work of God in the beauty of creation, in the colors of birds and the power of love a parent has for a newborn child. Gerson sees the transcendent God at work in these things, too, but he also credits his faith and the church for sustaining him in and through his darkest times. He recounts a time in 2002 when he found himself dissolving in tears and relief at the sight of a sculpture at the Cathedral depicting the Prodigal Son collapsed in his father's arms. In that moment he promised himself and God that he would be a better man, that he would stop focusing on himself so much of the time. He continues:

> I have failed at these goals in a disturbing variety of ways. And I have more doubts than I did on that day. These kinds of experiences may result from inspiration ... or indigestion. Your brain may be playing tricks. Or you may be feeling the beating heart of the universe. Faith, thankfully, does not preclude doubt. It consists of staking your life on the rumor of grace.[97]

It sounds almost like Paul, doesn't it? *Staking your life. I am convinced.* Why is it so difficult to trust that rumor? We are quick to believe other

---

[97] Gerson

rumors, the ones about conspiracies and dire plots, the ones that tell us the worst about a person or an institution. Why is it so hard on so many days to believe this "rumor of grace" is true?

In a moment we will welcome a new member into the Christ Presbyterian community. In the words we will use to make Leigh's membership official, you will hear me say, "remember your baptism and be thankful, and know that the Holy Spirit is at work within you."[98] Know that God's Spirit is at work in you. Trust the rumor of grace. Be convinced that the God we meet in Jesus Christ is at work in the world taking the mess that bombards us every day and creating something new and whole. These are not easy challenges; these convictions are not our default drive, at least left to my own devices they are not my default drive. And that is why we need this community to help each other trust the rumor to be true. It is too hard to trust it all on our own.

Last week, we were drawn back to the font where we are reminded of God's love poured out for us in Jesus Christ, "grace that interrupts the consequences of our actions," we were told.[99] Today we are called to the table, the place where we are welcomed to the joyful feast of the people of God. Paul is convinced that nothing can separate us from the love of God in Christ Jesus, but on so many days, God can seem far away and far removed. And yet in this sacrament, in this meal, we are invited to take and eat. In this meal we are reminded that in Jesus Christ God comes to us in the flesh, breaking down any division between the holy and the human. "Take, eat, this is my body given for you," Jesus tells his disciples. Paul insists that he is convinced that nothing, nothing in all creation—not even the very best we can experience or the worst we can endure—can separate us from God's love. And as we share the gift of the bread and the cup, as we feast on this meal—one we do not earn, one we cannot replace—we are

---

[98] From the PCUSA 2018 *Book of Common Worship*
[99] Bono, as cited in *Under Grace*, preached at CPC on May 26, 2019

strengthened for our work out in God's world. In this world God may feel faraway, but rest assured it is the very world God so dearly loves and has never abandoned. And God relies on us, yes, us, to live lives that give others a reason to believe that the "rumor of grace" is true. So as you prepare to take this meal, I invite you to think about and maybe even write down what you are convinced of here and now. Or maybe you need to ask God to convince you again that you are loved, that you are worthy of being saved. Because the rumor is true. For by the grace of God I am convinced that neither hatred, nor inadequacy, nor arrogance, nor racism, nor fear, nor violence, nor dementia, nor cancer, nor addiction, nor depression, nor apathy, nor life, nor death, nor anything in God's creation can separate us from the love of God in Christ Jesus our Lord. And I am convinced that in the midst of our detours and our doubts, our shortcomings and our overreaching, our God wants to convince us that nothing, not one thing can separate us from God's love made flesh in Jesus Christ. So come, share in the joyful feast given to us at this table, bask in the grace poured out for you, and know that you are immersed even now in the love that knows no bounds.

Thanks be to God. Amen.

One Small Step
1 Corinthians 12:12-27

July 21, 2019

Fifty years ago this past week, a human being took his first step on the moon, and Neil Armstrong's first words became the stuff of history. But apparently, we didn't really hear what he actually said. The quote we recall—the one touted in history books and on the news, is "That's one small step for man; one giant leap for mankind." In reality, Armstrong says he said, "That's one small step for (a) man; one giant leap for mankind."[100] Speech experts and other researchers have spent hours listening for that missing "a." Some hear it; others don't. But most agree that the "a" is implied, that Armstrong understood himself not as a lone ranger, superhero type, but as the one human being given the extraordinary opportunity to be the first to step on that faraway rocky terrain on behalf of all of us. He understood himself as part of a larger whole.

To use Paul's language, we might understand Armstrong and other heroes like him as part of the body, but maybe one of the better parts, like a strong arm or a swift leg, rather than say, an elbow or a knuckle or a belly button or a toenail. But that's just it. Paul wants to make sure that we all view ourselves as indispensable parts of a larger whole, no matter what our part may be, and that we view others as indispensable parts, too, no matter which parts they may be. This is an internal memo of sorts, a letter to the church at Corinth. That young church apparently had some pecking-order issues, some mistaken ideas that some members were more important than others. Paul wants to make it clear in no uncertain terms that baptism—that messy, wet, public welcome into Christ's church—is the great equalizer, that in our being

---

[100] https://time.com/5621999/neil-armstrong-quote/

brought into Christ's church, in being made part of his body, we are all equally indispensable, crucial to God's mission in and for the world.

Joanne Thompson, Lillie Elliott, Ruth Anna Ratledge, and Anna Lee Minner were seamstresses who worked in a factory owned by Playtex, also known as International Latex Corporation in Dover, Delaware. Before their company signed a contract with NASA, they spent their days sewing undergarments, including girdles. After the NASA project came online, these women were part of the crew who cut the patterns and stitched every stitch of the spacesuits the astronauts wore. The seamstresses got to know the astronauts through personal visits for fittings and through the photos of the men's faces that hung with each suit. They knew that the men's lives were in their hands. Their careful attention to each stitch ensured the astronauts' safety as they headed into the great unknown:

> Seamstress Joanne Thompson said, 'We would have astronauts come in and thank us, and that was a real boost. It made a connection there that you didn't forget.'

> And on July 20, 1969, when the big moment finally arrived, the women of International Latex held their breath. Lillie Elliott recalled, 'Once they started down the ladder, and he put his foot on the moon, that was a pinnacle of watching something that you've helped do.'[101]

Every spacesuit they created worked beautifully; not one failed to keep an astronaut safe. Their work never made headlines or got top billing, but their work was indispensable; they were indispensable to the larger mission.

---

[101] https://www.cbsnews.com/news/apollo-11-the-seamstresses-who-helped-put-a-man-on-the-moon/

Do you realize that you are indispensable to the body of Christ? Do you realize that everyone who shares your baptism is also indispensable to the body of Christ? I'm not sure which of those questions is harder to answer, but I think they are crucial questions for us to consider because they get to the very heart of who we are called to be as a community, as Christ's body in and for the world.

Later this morning, we will spend some time working on projects for neighbors nearby and faraway. We will likely never know their names or their stories, and yet the time, the prayers, the energy, the intention, and the work you offer is indispensable to the larger mission God calls us to. Assembling a Welcome Home Kit, making cards or creating tray decorations for Meals on Wheels, rolling sweatpants for Project ASK, preparing supplies for Dress A Girl kits: all of these seemingly small acts make a real difference in the lives of friends and strangers. We need you; we need each other to accomplish the mission, but your being indispensable goes far beyond these activities. Your being indispensable extends beyond this one day. You are members, we are members—limbs, the Greek tells us—of the body of Christ. You ARE. Y'all are. All y'all are. All of us, young, old, fast, slow, happy, grumpy, grieving the past, lamenting the present, or excited about the future. All of us. We ARE now members of the body of Christ. There is no opt out clause, no exceptions to the rule. Whether you are a strong shoulder or the daintiest pinky toe or something in between, you are indispensable to the body of Christ, as is your pew mate, as are our brothers and sisters worshipping in sanctuaries around the corner, across the river, and around the world. We may not always agree on what kind of music we should sing or the role of women or politics or plans for a way forward in this divided moment. We differ in so many ways, but that does not seem to bother Paul. In his moment and in ours, I get the sense that he is concerned with how we view ourselves and one another inside the church. God still has big hopes for the body of Christ. God still counts on us to bring God's radical love in Jesus

Christ to a world in desperate need of loving, saving, and redeeming, and God expects us to be the ones to do that work, to help pull off that mission. But if Paul is to be believed, we have some homework, some bodywork to do first. How we work with and welcome the great and the not-so-great, the beautiful and the less-than-perfect as a community and as individuals shapes us at a fundamental level. We are members—arms, legs, hands, feet, elbows, toenails, and kneecaps—indispensable parts one and all in the body of Christ. And they are, too.

The women who stitched those first spacesuits are retired now, but they would do it again in a heartbeat:

> 'We enjoyed every bit of it, every stitch. I would do it all over again if I could,' said Ruth Anna Ratledge...
>
> 'You'd still like to be doin' it?' asked [interviewer Tracey] Smith
>
> 'Yes,' she laughed. 'I loved it.'
>
> Joanne Thompson added, 'Wow, I'm still amazed, it was great!'
>
> ...ILC is still making spacesuits ... and who knows? An ILC suit might one day go to Mars. But it all began with Apollo 11, and a small group of dedicated women back on Earth who helped bring us all just a little closer to the heavens.[102]

Isn't that our calling, too, to reflect God's love to one another and the world? We cannot save ourselves, nor can we save one another, but we can show one another the love of Christ, and we can live that love in the world. In that sense—each and every member, each and every part, each and every limb—can do our indispensable, irreplaceable bit, our one small step toward drawing one another just a little closer to the

---

[102] https://www.cbsnews.com/news/apollo-11-the-seamstresses-who-helped-put-a-man-on-the-moon/

heavens. And by the grace of God, we will find ourselves stitched more closely to each other and to Christ himself without ever leaving planet earth.

In the name of the Father and of the Son and of the Holy Spirit. Amen.

Red Boots and Reconciliation
2 Corinthians 5: 11-21

July 10, 2016

Out of the whole of 2 Corinthians, this text is probably the most familiar with its wonderful words about the old life's being gone and a new life begun. Paul's words about reconciliation and our being ambassadors for Christ are some of the most winsome words in all of scripture. So all of this is to say, I was so looking forward to preaching on this text, and then this week happened. Senseless killing of black men in Baton Rouge and St. Paul were followed by the senseless killing of police officers in Dallas. Laments and debates and anger and fear swirl around us. Despair threatens to drown out hope and reason and even faith.

And then by the grace of God and through the work of the Spirit, Paul speaks to me again through these ancient words. I mentioned in bible study this week that I have grown quite fond of Paul. In our time with Paul and the Corinthian church, I have gained a deeper appreciation for Paul—not for him the biblical superhero, but for the Paul the man of deep faith who is "[urged] on by the love of Christ."[103] It's not that Paul is perfect; it's not that he has no agenda; it's that his agenda is God's agenda as revealed in Christ. Paul repeatedly steps into the fray, into the divisions with one and only one agenda: to share the love of Christ. This love is the foundation of his work with the Corinthians. Paul understands his work to be the ministry of reconciliation, the work of bridging gaps and bringing healing between factions. While he may agree with one side more than another, he sets aside his own bias. He hears a call to shift how we see one another, to look at others not from a human point of view but from God's point of view. Like us, Paul longs for a world where we will not need to cry out that black

---

[103] 2 Corinthians 5: 14, NRSV

141

lives matter or that blue lives matter, because in the kingdom of God and from God's point of view, all lives are treasured, all lives matter, but the world around Paul was not there yet. The world around us is not there yet either. It's not that black lives or blue lives or gay lives or brown lives or refugee lives or certain Corinthian lives matter *more*. It's that they matter, *too*, but their mattering is not all that evident in Paul's world or ours.[104] A world where all lives truly matter is the world Paul envisions and longs for. That's the world he feels called to help usher in. So he steps into the fray and offers words of hope and healing. We are a new creation, he reminds us. We broken and fragile and treasured clay pots have been given new hope and new life by the Holy Potter, our Creator. We are freed and forgiven in the name of the One who died on a cross—the worst execution the Romans had at their disposal—for all. In response, like Paul, we are called to live for Christ, to be his representatives in the world. Piece of cake, right?

Early in the spring of my sophomore year of high school, my ballet teacher sent home some information about costumes for the spring concert. My mother did not sew, nor do I, so we were relieved when we saw that the only thing I needed was a pair of red boots. Mrs. Hamilton gave specific instructions about which boots to purchase and where. They were short flat, red suede boots, and I thought they were fantastic, but to dance in? We had rubber soles put on the bottoms and trusted where Mrs. Hamilton led. With her faithful help and choreography, I twirled in those boots and kicked and leaped in those boots. I also fell flat on my face in those boots and got terrible shin splints in those boots, and when that happened, Mrs. Hamilton was the first one on the scene to reassure me, to remind me that I knew the steps, and to send me back on stage to twirl and kick and leap once more. I loved the boots because of where they took me, because of who I was when I wore them. With Mrs. Hamilton just off-stage, I felt

---

104 Thanks to David Lamotte for giving me the words.

brave in those boots, able to step on the stage and be the dancer I longed to be all the time—on stage and off.

Because of my affection for those boots (and my ridiculous love of shoes in general), I was intrigued when I started seeing mentions of the Red Boot Coalition earlier this year. My first thought was, "These are my people!" After reading a bit more, I found myself hoping and praying I was right:

> The idea started by accident and in a very small, quiet kind of way. In 2010, Molly Barker, founder of Girls on the Run International, gave a TEDx presentation where she began the speech with an innocent-enough story about a pair of...yep, you guessed it...red boots.
>
> Molly, a self-proclaimed 'bad dresser' and 'fashion nightmare,' would have never considered wearing something so bold as red boots. 'Fifty-year-old women do not wear red boots,' she recounts the story in her speech. Molly's daughter Helen disagreed; and so she purchased a pair of the 'youthful' boots and presented them to her mom for her 50th birthday.
>
> Molly wore them to her TEDx talk and so began the red boot journey. Since the historic wearing of the red boots, Molly can't go anywhere without someone asking about those darn boots. She has received hundreds of red boot tales from countless men and women. Pictures of red boots started showing up on her Facebook page and in emails...most accompanied by a tale or two of how *my red-boots got me through--you name it--mothers dying, chemotherapy, divorces, the death of a child, first jobs, first dates, coming out, retiring, growing old and having babies*—to name a few.[105]

---

[105] http://theredbootcoalition.org/our-story

Molly found inspiration from these red boot tales and thought she might be on to something. She courageously embraced the challenge of working with others to bring some compassion and hope to conversations inside Washington. Along the way she stumbled over roadblocks and stepped on political landmines. She felt defeated and frustrated. She no longer smiled at strangers, and she grew wary about raising her voice. She began to doubt that her efforts mattered. The initiative failed, and Molly sought to re-group. People from all over offered encouragement and hope, so Molly took herself and her boots on a road trip across the country:

> In August of 2014, she drove from Charlotte to Las Vegas and back, interviewing hundreds of Americans about our nation's conversations on politics, religion, race, sexuality, gender and economics.[106]

She learned a lot and wanted to find a way to birth similar conversations around the country. So Molly came up with a plan. She outlined eleven steps that read like a covenant or a set of ground rules. The first one states:

> We came to see that, despite sometimes feeling helpless, angry and even apathetic about the current course of human events, we each play an essential role in our communities, our families, and our lives. **We matter.**[107]

The other steps include being trusting, open, joyful, grateful, and engaged. Small groups gather in coffee shops and jails and offices and community rooms and mosques and churches and begin talking, sharing, and—perhaps most importantly—listening, not arguing, not browbeating, not persuading, not debating, but listening. Slowly, walls are coming down and bridges are being built; slowly relationships are

---

[106] http://theredbootcoalition.org/our-story
[107] http://theredbootcoalition.org/the-11-steps

being restored; slowly and sometimes clumsily, trust is being repaired, person by person, conversation by conversation. This is the ministry Paul describes. This is the dance of reconciliation work.

And it all begins with that first step: We matter. We matter enough for God to save us again and again and again. We matter enough for Christ to be born as one of us and to live among us, eating with prostitutes, kissing lepers, confronting the powers, and welcoming children. We matter enough for Christ to die a criminal's death for us. We matter enough for Christ to raise us to new life with him. We matter. Corinthian lives matter, black lives matter, blue lives matter, white lives matter, gay lives matter, rich lives matter, straight lives matter, brown lives matter, young lives matter, refugee lives matter, and poor lives matter. Christ died for all, because from Christ's point of view, we all matter. We should know this. The world should know this, but somewhere along the way, I'm afraid we have all forgotten, or we have simply refused to believe it in our core. So we need to be reminded: we matter beyond measure. We all matter. Once that reminder sinks in, once we believe it, it becomes time for us to do some reminding ourselves. Corinth needed reminding then; the world desperately needs reminding now. And we're the ones called to do that reminding work, that reconciliation work together.

We are not simply invited or encouraged to do this work; we are called to do this work. By virtue of our being raised to new life in Christ, like Paul, we are all already ambassadors. It's our job. **We** have been entrusted with this great good news: the old life is gone; a new life has begun. This ambassador work is not a desk job. The world is crying out for this reconciliation dance. The time is now. The curtain has gone up. We cannot remain silent. We are not called to stand in the wings or critique from the audience. We are standing on stage. We now have to take that first step. We may have to repeat that first step again and again. We matter. Everyone matters. We need to hear it, we need to believe it, and then we need to speak it and live it. It's a huge risk, and it won't always be pretty. There will be days when we will blow it. We will be uncomfortable. We will get shin splints and blisters. We will get the steps wrong. We will step on toes. Our egos will get wounded. We may even fall flat on our faces. But by the grace of God, there will also be days when we do get it right, days when we'll fall into step with new dance partners and learn new choreography. There will be days when we soar, days when we twirl and leap with joy. And with every step, the God we meet in Jesus Christ will be there to pick us up when we fall, to encourage us, to challenge us, to usher us back on stage, and to dance with us, all of us in the kingdom of God.

Thanks be to God. Amen.

Rainy Days and Mr. Rogers
Galatians 5, selected verses

July 22, 2018

When was the last time you wrote a letter? An actual letter, with a pen and stationery, a stamp and an envelope? I'm not sure I could name the last time I wrote one, but I have an entire folder filled with ones I have received. They are kept in what I call my "rainy day" file, a file of notes, letters, and other bits and pieces that I can pull out when it's been a long day or a hard week. The words and images shine a ray of light into the occasional rainy day, make me smile, give me hope, and encourage me to keep doing what I believe I've been called to do, even on the hard days—maybe especially on the hard days.

Paul could use a rainy-day file. He is writing the churches at Galatia out of love and out of anger and frustration. He has shared the gospel with them and now fears that they are falling for a twisted form of the gospel, one that demands circumcision in order to be a full-fledged member of the body of Christ. He has proclaimed grace to them, but now he fears they are trading grace for something else, buying in to a false gospel that divides the community into pieces. We tend to think of Paul and the early church as being solid, faithful, passionate, and confident—or at least I do. And yet, as many of Paul's letters reveal, the church is fickle, fragile and fractious from her earliest moments, not because God or God's grace in Jesus Christ is fickle or fragile or fractious, but because we are. We want something to hang on to; we insist on wanting some control over what happens to us—and to others. Jumping through hoops, checking off certain tasks gives human beings a sense that we can control our lives and our salvation. When Paul rants about our selfish desires, he's lamenting our stubborn insistence on relying on our strength, our accomplishments, our abilities, our paycheck, our family name, our GPA, our address, or our

IRA for our salvation instead of God. He worries that the Galatians' determination to follow a gospel that hinges on human works undermines the true gospel of Christ, the true freedom found in Christ, and undermines the body of Christ itself. He worries because he is seeing it—or at least hearing about—the fraying of the new Christian community in real time. In a list that would make any bible-thumping preacher rub her hands together with glee, Paul lists all the things that tear at a community when it becomes focused on me and mine, on what you've done, on what I want. We tend to giggle at the more eyebrow-raising items on the list, but it's the more run-of-the-mill ones that caught my attention this past week: "hate, fighting, obsession, losing your temper, competitive opposition, conflict, selfishness, group rivalry, jealousy."[108] These caught my attention because we are seeing these very behaviors play out in real time here and now. We hear hate and selfishness and rivalry shouted from both sides of the aisle, both sides of the river, and all corners of the world by people who claim to worship the very same God we do, and sadly sometimes even in the name of that God. I get it. It is tempting. When I see families torn apart in the name of justice and human beings demeaned in the name of freedom under the guise of living in a Christian nation, my stomach turns. I am the first one to mutter words I shouldn't and to think things about "them" that are far from faithful or good or loving or kind. And it is then when I realize I am checking things off the wrong list. I am failing to trust the Spirit that works in and through me, giving those around me little to write home about, and offering the world very little for its rainy-day file on behalf of the One who saves me. Because that is who we are called and shaped to be, right? While Paul's letter is directed very specifically to the church, he also recognizes how broken our witness becomes when we fail to reflect the Christ who claims us and sends us out to share the Good News with a hurting world.

---

[108] Galatians 5:20-21, CEB

One of you recently told me I couldn't talk about Mr. Rogers anymore because any and all mention of him makes you tear up. Makes me tear up, too, but I'm hoping you'll indulge me once more because Mr. Rogers is very much a thing right now. *Won't You Be My Neighbor?*, the recent documentary about him recently passed the $10 million mark, making it the most successful documentary of 2018 thus far. And no one is more astonished by its success than Morgan Neville, the filmmaker behind the film. But he suspects the success reflects something about our present moment. Simply stated, "We need Mr. Rogers."[109] Clearly, the film has tapped into more than nostalgia for a slow-talking, cardigan-wearing Presbyterian preacher from Pittsburgh. I wonder if it has tapped into our longing to live in a different Spirit than the one that seems to have grabbed hold of our nation and our world.

And yet it's not all bad news all the time. There are good news stories out there, tales of people showing us what generosity, kindness, patience, and faith look like, feel like, and sound like. There's Kylian Mbappe, the World Cup star who grew up in a diverse but poor suburb of Paris. Mbappe is giving the entirety of his winnings from the World Cup to a charity that offers sports opportunities for children who are hospitalized or disabled.[110] This is the Spirit's work of generosity on display. There's a Secret Santa program in Kansas City, Missouri where police officers pull over vehicles with dents or a broken taillights and hand out cash gifts to the drivers rather than tickets, inspiring hugs and tears from parents who had been choosing the right words to explain the lack of gifts under the non-existent tree.[111] It's hard to imagine a better image of the Spirit's joy at work. Or there's an innovative

---

[109] https://www.redletterchristians.org/the-surprising-success-faith-of-wont-you-be-my-neighbor/

[110] https://www.cnn.com/2018/07/17/football/kylian-mbappe-france-croatia-world-cup-final-spt-intl/index.html

[111] https://www.cbsnews.com/news/sheriffs-deputies-kindness-brings-drivers-to-tears/

nonprofit in Nashville called Shower Up. Their mission is "to build relationships, restore hope and dignity, and show the love of God with those in need by providing them with shower services and personal care."[112] They have several mobile shower trucks that they take to places where homeless men and women are known to congregate. They offer hot showers, good meals, and haircuts provided by professionals who donate their time and skills to help some of the neediest Nashvillians. And that is one prime example of the Spirit's work of kindness. These are just a few examples of people who are reflecting that different Spirit, God's Spirit, but perhaps those stories—or our sharing of those stories or the Spirit they reflect is all too rare, because they get drowned out by the incessant and relentless examples of all that flows from that other spirit, the spirit of selfishness, anger, hatred, and greed.

Perhaps the most poignant moment in *Won't You Be My Neighbor?* — spoiler alert—comes at the end when the filmmaker riffs on words Rogers offered in commencement speeches and at award shows. He asks each person interviewed for the film to pause for a full minute and think about someone who had "loved them into loving, smiled them into smiling," who had encouraged these men and women into becoming who they are. And for a full, silent minute we watch through tears along with the people on the screen as they reflect—on the someone—or someones—who come to mind. I'd like to add another to that list. Who comes to mind when I ask not only who has smiled you into smiling, or who has loved you into loving, but also who has believed you into believing? Who has shared the power of God's grace with you? Who has shown you what it is to live by the Spirit? I'll give you a moment to think. And, like Mr. Rogers, I'll watch the time.[113]

---

[112] http://www.showerup.org/
[113] One of the best examples can be found here:
https://www.youtube.com/watch?v=TcNxY4TudXo

My hope is that you imagined words and faces of people who have shown you kindness, who have given you joy, who have taught you patience or self-control, who have embodied goodness, faithfulness, and peace for you. This is the stuff of rainy-day files on a cosmic scale. It is this kind of life and witness the church is called to exhibit to the world. These are the fruits; this is the Spirit we are called to nurture in one another. Paul does not come to us wearing a cardigan or comfortable sneakers, but he does come to us with a call for the church to lean not on our own successes or our own achievements but on the gift of grace and on our Savior, Jesus Christ. This is not easy. This is not the stuff of flowers or rainbows or unicorns or the occasional random act of kindness. These fruits, this Spirit is essential to who we are and how we are as the Body of Christ—not just on Sundays, but every day, rainy or not. Paul calls the Galatians and us to be a radical people who resist the call to demean and disgrace those who are different from us, people who refuse to cast off the littlest and the least, people who find a way to stand firm in the face of hatred spewed for shock value and ratings and self-preservation. Instead Paul calls us to choose a different way, to overflow with the fruit the Spirit, to share the love, joy, peace, patience, kindness, goodness, faithfulness, gentleness, and self-control embodied in our beloved Savior with one another and with a world that seems determined to go its own way. No, the world will never know another cardigan-wearing, puppet-wielding Fred Rogers who fills our rainy-day files with songs of encouragement or messages of love, but by the grace of God, we have each other and by the call of the Spirit, the world has us. So maybe it's time to find our cardigans, to lace up our sneakers, and to offer up the fruit others have so faithfully nurtured in us.

In the name of the Father and the Son and the Holy Spirit. Amen.

Stand

Revelation 5

August 13, 2017

Last week we followed John, the visionary writer of Revelation as he was invited through an open door that led into the heavenly throne room. Through John's eyes we found ourselves in the midst of worship with every creature bowing in praise of the one on the throne. Today we are still with John in that throne room waiting to see what happens next. Again it is a vivid scene packed with images and pictures. If you are comfortable doing so, I invite you to close your eyes and imagine the scene John paints as I read. Let us listen for what the Spirit is saying to the church in Revelation chapter 5. [Read Revelation 5.]

Summer is the time for superheroes, and this one has been no different. I grew up with Christopher Reeve playing Superman. "Super Friends" was one of my favorite Saturday morning cartoons. And who didn't want to fly in Wonder Woman's invisible jet? More recently I haven't been as enamored with Batman or Superman. I can't tell you much about Captain America or the Flash. I haven't seen the new Spiderman movie. But I did make a point of seeing *Wonder Woman*, and for the first time in decades I am tempted to dress up for Halloween. After growing up in a divine and protected world, Diana or Wonder Woman, finds herself in the middle of World War I. She does everything in her power to protect the vulnerable and confront evil as she seeks to bring an end to that war and all wars. Alongside a rag tag group of mercenaries, she makes her way to the front lines. In one scene, wielding only her shield, she storms across the battlefield defending herself from German gunfire in order to liberate a village held hostage by enemy forces. In this one scene, she never fires a bullet, she never pulls out her sword, but she puts herself in harm's way to help the hurting and the hungry. At one point in the movie she is asked why she does this because she has been told from infancy that humanity does not deserve her or any sacrifice she might make on her behalf. She responds, "It's not about deserve. It's about what you believe. And I believe in love." So the world gets another superhero, but maybe not the one we expect.

In this second scene in the heavenly throne room, John begins to weep because no one is worthy to open the scroll God holds. Most scholars argue that:

> The seven-sealed scroll holds the details about the plan and purpose of human history. [If this is the case], then the one charged to open and read it is the one given charge of that history.[114]

Almost immediately, one of the elders reassures John that there is One who can open the scroll. That One is "the lion of the tribe of Judah." So we are primed to expect the king of the beasts with a loud roar and a flowing mane. Instead, we are greeted by a lamb, and a slaughtered one at that. This is not the Savior we expect. He has seven horns and seven eyes. The seven horns point to his power. The seven eyes point to his wisdom. The number seven "symbolizes wholeness, fullness, completion."[115] The Lamb's wisdom and power are complete and perfect. This Savior, this promised Messiah, this all-wise and perfect Lamb is standing in the midst of the throne and the elders. We expect a lion and we get a Lamb, and it is he who is worthy to open the scroll and to take charge of the word it reveals. He is worthy because of his death. He is worthy because of his witness.

New Testament scholar Brian Blount wants us to grasp the full power of this image. The Lamb, Jesus Christ is "God's prime witness," the

---

[114] Brian Blount, *Revelation: A Commentary*, The New Testament Library (Louisville: Westminster John Knox, 2009) 96.
[115] Blount, 112.

very One who suffered and died because of his witnessing, because of his testifying to God's lordship.[116] John writes in the shadow of the Roman Empire. He has been exiled to the island of Patmos. He is where he is "because of the word of God and the testimony [or witness] of Jesus."[117] The communities to whom he writes are also in the shadow of the empire. A choice lies before them: play it safe and go along with the empire or testify to the lordship of Jesus Christ and risk persecution and even death. Clearly, John has chosen a side. He chooses to stand with Jesus in opposition to an empire that wants his loyalty. In this vision he sees the Lamb who stands with him. The language John uses to describe the Lamb's standing carries a note of resistance: "He appears to mean something like 'standing up' or 'standing fast.'" Blount goes on to say that the Lamb's "posture is itself one of resurrected defiance—a powerful hopeful message for a people who fear that their own witness" may result in persecution.[118] This is not Mary's little lamb. This is the Lamb of God who has confronted and resisted the powers before, who defiantly continues to resist them now.

John's language about *where* the Lamb stands is significant, too. The text tells us that John sees the Lamb "between the throne and the four living creatures and among the elders."[119] Blount points out that:

> If the elders represent the outer ring of the throne room attendees and the cherubim the innermost ring, the Messianic figure John sees cannot be in the midst of both groups at the same time. John's language therefore suggests movement. The one who is worthy is in effect 'working' the throne room. He

---

116 Blount, 110.
117 Revelation 1:9, NRSV
118 Blount, 111.
119 Revelation 5:6, NRSV

is on the move, next to God…and yet also in the midst of the…believers, who witness to God's lordship.[120]

So this Lamb does not stand by or stay still. He is not posing for a picture; he is on the move. This slain Lamb, this resurrected One is moving in and amongst the faithful and by God's side as well. And this one has saved saints—faithful ones—from "every tribe and language and people and nation; [and] made them to be a kingdom and priests serving God."[121] In other words—at the risk of sounding like Captain Obvious—in his death and resurrection, this Lamb, this Christ has created a community to serve God in his name, a community called to live and witness in a particular way, a community called to be on the move as well.

One other hero in the Wonder Woman movie is Steve Trevor. I don't remember much about his character in the TV show in the seventies, but this one is another unlikely hero. He seems to be a bit of a rebel, a loner who works as a spy. But there is something noble in him, too. Early in the movie he recalls a lesson his father shared with him:

> My father told me once, 'if you see something wrong happening in the world, you can either do nothing, or you can do something.' And I already tried nothing.[122]

If we claim the one who has claimed us, if we are in fact part of members of that "kingdom and priests serving God," we too have that choice before us: nothing or something. Sadly, I for one have tried a version of nothing. I have worried and wrung my hands about poverty, about racism, about failing schools, about the insidiousness of white supremacy. Over the course of the past week, I followed news stories about the mounting tensions in Charlottesville, Virginia and the

---

[120] Blount, 108.

[121] Revelation 5:9

[122] https://www.hypable.com/wonder-woman-quotes-inspire/

expected rally planned for this weekend. I worried and wrung my hands about it, too. I've prayed, too. And hear me clearly: prayer is not nothing—far from it—but in the face of hatred and racism and white supremacy, prayer is not enough. If I believe that the God I meet in Jesus is on the move, risking his life to stand up and stand fast against the powers of hatred and fear and division and oppression, then that is what I am called to do as well. And not only when there's a televised rally happening down the road.

I read an article written by two graduates of UVA this past week. Martese Johnson graduated in 2016 from the University of Virginia with a bachelor's degree in Italian studies. Aryn Frazier graduated from UVA this year with a bachelor's in African American and African studies. In March 2015, Johnson, who is African American, was bloodied during an arrest outside a Charlottesville bar that drew widespread attention amid national debate about race and law enforcement. Frazier was a leader in the U-Va. Black Student Alliance and participated in protests over how Johnson was treated. In their column they suggest that yesterday's rally itself is not as important as we might think:

> This is not because blatant demonstrations of hate no longer matter in 2017 — the rationale is actually quite the opposite. The very existence of the KKK, the hatred for which it stands, and the vitriol that its members spew is absolutely important. It is important because it reminds people that, for as far as we've come and as many minds as have been changed, we still have quite a long way to go.[123]

They go on to explain that their deeper concern is about the subtle and pernicious ways racism is at work not simply in the outrageous acts

---

[123] https://www.washingtonpost.com/news/grade-point/wp/2017/08/08/why-the-upcoming-alt-right-rally-in-charlottesville-may-be-less-important-than-we-think/

that draw media attention, but also in the everyday world in which we live, the world where black parents have to teach their children how to respond when they encounter a police officer. It's called "the talk," and it's unlike any talk I have had to have with my daughter. This same world sees disproportionate poverty among people of color. Black and brown children are more likely to attend failing schools. This world laughs off jokes about "those people" and generalizations about "their kind." This same world balks when people say, "Black lives matter." It is not that black lives somehow matter more than white lives; it's that we live in a world that does not seem to think they matter much at all. This is the world in which we live, **and** this is the world where the saints Christ saves are called to love and serve God.

As I worked and re-worked this sermon last night and this morning, I found myself weeping like John. I found myself wishing for a superhero to swoop in and make it all better, but even Wonder Woman cannot do that. And we don't need a superhero. By the grace of God, I am, we are saints saved by Jesus Christ to be a kingdom and priests from **every** tribe and language and people and nation serving God. Our blessed Savior is the Lamb who was slain for testifying that there is only one Lord, only one King. We may not deserve him, but he came in love for us, and he died for our sake, to save us—and all—from anything and everything that would separate us from God and from each other. He stands up for us and calls us to stand with him against the powers, against the voices that shout fear, against the systems that sow division, against the hatred that compels someone to drive a car into a crowd. I don't know what all the steps are, but maybe the first step is to stand up and to find the courage to stand where Christ stands. It's far more faithful than doing nothing.

In the name of the Father and of the Son and of the Holy Spirit. Amen.

CPSIA information can be obtained
at www.ICGtesting.com
Printed in the USA
BVHW040035241219
567685BV00011BA/132/P